Studies in Social Ecology and Pathology
General Editor: NIGEL WALKER

Freedom and Justice within Walls

Freedom and Justice within Walls
THE BRISTOL PRISON EXPERIMENT

F. E. Emery

TAVISTOCK PUBLICATIONS
London · New York · Sydney · Toronto · Wellington

First published in 1970
By Tavistock Publications Limited
11 New Fetter Lane, London E.C.4
Printed in Great Britain
In 10 point Times New Roman
By Cox and Wyman Limited
Fakenham, Norfolk

SBN 422 73300 8

Distributed in the USA
by Barnes & Noble, Inc.

Contents

Preface

When someone finds time to write a full and objective history of the English prison system in the first hundred years after its nationalization, I hope that he will emphasize two phenomena. One is the comparative neglect of the problems of the 'local prisons' – that is, the 'receiving prisons' which have to cope with the miscellany of sentenced, remanded, and civil prisoners whom the courts entrust to their care. The creation of borstals, open prisons, training prisons, and other specialized establishments in the first half of this century inevitably diverted both resources and attention in those directions; and innovations are always more exciting than improvements.

The other phenomenon is the difficulty and reluctance with which certain assumptions were abandoned. One of these was that association between prisoners was inherently undesirable. The origins of this belief, which underlay the 'separate system' and the 'silent system', were not wholly irrational, however extreme these systems were. It was a recognition of the importance of what sociologists would now call 'the inmate subculture of the total institution', and it was an attempt to protect the unsophisticated criminal from this influence. Solitary confinement was of course a crude prophylactic, and it was not long before its ill-effects were recognized; but the 'rule of silence' survived longer. In 1900, when – as part of the Gladstone Committee's reforms – prisons were instructed to allow conversation between prisoners at exercise, the reactions in governors' reports were almost entirely unfavourable: 'Conversation at exercise is only appreciated by the habitual criminal.' 'Conversation at exercise is not sought after; prisoners prefer to exercise in the usual way.'[1] Even as late as 1952, when the Chairman of the Prison Commission said that the rule of silence no longer existed in English prisons,[2] he went on to explain that 'talking is restricted, though not forbidden, on certain

[1] From the Prison Commissioners' Annual Report for 1900.
[2] Sir Lionel Fox. *The English Prison and Borstal System*, London, Routledge and Kegan Paul, 1952, p. 160.

occasions, and entirely unrestricted on others. During working hours, gossip and unnecessary chatter will be discouraged, as also when parties of prisoners are moving about under supervision . . .'.

Another assumption was that relations between staff and prisoners should be formal. In theory, if not always in practice, communication between officers and ordinary prisoners was restricted to the exchange of instructions and essential information. The officer who 'fraternized' did so at the risk of disapproval and even reprimand from his superiors. If he kept in touch with a prisoner after the latter's discharge he risked a disciplinary charge. Like the 'silent system', this prohibition, of course, had its rational aspect. The less communication between prisoner and staff, the less corruption of staff. Even innocent but inessential communication wastes time and creates problems which interfere with the smooth running of large custodial establishments. A wholly rational calculation, of course, would have taken into account the lost opportunities and the positive damage that also resulted; and the fact that it took so long to recognize these must be attributed to irrational motivation of kinds which are too obvious – and natural – to need discussion here.

The process of relaxation began with the borstals and the prisons where the men were serving medium or long sentences. It was understandable that it took longer to reach the 'locals', since these have always suffered from several kinds of difficulty. Their population is extremely heterogeneous, and includes – or included – debtors, men awaiting trial, men under psychiatric observation, men awaiting transfer to regional or central prisons, men sent to the local for 'accumulated visits' by relatives, and of course the miscellany of men who spend the whole of a short sentence in the local for drunkenness, vagrancy, homosexual behaviour, petty dishonesty, or violence. The short time for which most of these men are in the local prison makes it very difficult for staff to establish more than superficial communication with them, and the difficulty is aggravated by the variety of their problems and personalities. Moreover, certain categories of prisoner must be segregated, not only to satisfy the official distinctions between tried and untried, civil and criminal, 'star' and 'ordinary', young and adult prisoners, but also because prisoners themselves draw distinctions which, if ignored, lead to friction and violence. Finally, the architecture of our locals, nearly all of which were built in the second half of the nineteenth century, when segregation was at its height, does not lend itself to informal association between small, manageable groups.

This may explain why it was not until the middle of the nineteen-fifties that the change of attitude towards communication in English custodial establishments can really be said to have penetrated to local prisons. It is an indication of the caution with which it was received that it began in a small local prison in the provinces, and was called the 'Norwich experiment'. The features of this experiment, as they were described in the Prison Commissioners' annual report for 1956, do not sound very startling nowadays. They were: 'dining in association for all convicted prisoners; increasing labour hours from 26 to 35 hours a week without increasing staff; and an attempt to improve the officer–prisoner relationship by allocating groups of prisoners to specific officers'. In the workshops, officers were encouraged to move about, instead of sitting on raised platforms (which were removed), and not only to allow more conversation between prisoners but also 'to have no qualms about having a helpful conversation' with prisoners themselves. As the governor said in his first report on this innovation, 'It is obviously taking time for this change in outlook to sink in amongst prisoners. Occasionally one enters a workshop to find an officer talking to a prisoner openly and amicably, only for the prisoner to give a quick warning look to the officer and then resume his work with excessive vigour.'

The governor's report, however, was so encouraging that governors of other small provincial 'locals' were sent to see the experiment in operation, with the result that the next year Shrewsbury, Swansea, and Oxford followed suit, in spite of staffing shortages. What had been the 'Norwich experiment' was now the 'Norwich system'. By the following year six more locals had either adopted it or were on the point of doing so. Some of these were larger establishments – although none approached the size of the huge London prisons – and the Commission seems to have felt that it was time for an appraisal. The decision to seek the help of the Tavistock Institute of Human Relations to take part in this appraisal was itself an indication of the change of outlook which was taking place. It was about this time that Terence and Pauline Morris were given permission to begin their famous study on Pentonville, the big London local.[1] Now the

[1] See Morris T. and Morris, P., *Pentonville*, London, Routledge and Kegan Paul, 1963.

Commission were not merely allowing access to an outside research team; they were inviting it.

Dr Emery, who had recently joined the Tavistock Institute as one of their senior social scientists, had a wide experience of research in human relations in other types of community or organization. The advantage of this should be obvious, but is often underestimated. As I have pointed out in another context,[1] the investigator who studies only one organization is apt to interpret phenomena as pathological when a comparative study would have shown him that they are endemic among all organizations of the kind. What do they know of prisons who only prisons know? Although Dr Emery does not draw explicit comparisons, it is obvious throughout his book that his acquaintance with the dynamics of other types of community and organization enabled him to see in perspective what might otherwise have assumed exaggerated importance.

Another merit of his approach is that he tries to understand – and to make understandable – the attitudes and conduct of the staff as well as of the prisoners. In a sense both prisoners and officers are captives within an institution which was designed by neither. The restraints on the behaviour of the officers are less tangible, but none the less real. Some books tell us why prisoners act and feel as they do; a very few books tell us why staff react to prisoners as they do: but Dr Emery makes the interaction intelligible – and with virtually none of the moral judgements which are implicit in so many descriptions of custodial institutions. This may help to explain his apparent success in overcoming the sensitivity of his subjects – a problem which confronts all such investigations, but is especially acute in prisons.

Another difficult task must have been to achieve the right mixture of quantification and impressionism. After all, though he has given us a valuable insight into the working of a local prison, his real assignment was to compare the state of the prison before and after the introduction of the Norwich system. Obviously, the more aspects of prison life he could quantify the better (not forgetting the danger that the easier something is to quantify the less it reflects what one really wants to measure). But figures without interpretation are useless, and interpretation without a certain amount of impressionism is impossible. Dr Emery manages to blend the three in nice proportions.

His report was, not surprisingly, favourable to the new system,

[1] *Morale in the Civil Service*, Edinburgh, Edinburgh University Press, 1961.

which is now the accepted form of regime in almost all English prisons, although shortage of officers and overcrowding of prisoners have meant that here and there it is hard to see more than a pale reflection of Norwich. As the final chapter points out, however, the new approach creates problems of its own. One may not agree that all these problems are real. Is it really true, for instance, that a closed prison must be inimical to any degree of inmate self-government? This may be so in a local prison, but because of its high turnover of inmates rather than its security. Nevertheless, some of Dr Emery's prophecies and recommendations have come to pass. The rapid spread of 'group counselling' in the early sixties involved a large number of basic-grade officers in a new role, which did indeed create tensions as well as disappointments of exaggerated expectations; and group counselling is now on the wane. All grades of staff now pay more attention to 'welfare', although the extent to which this is attributable to improved staff–inmate communication is difficult to assess. In some prisons welfare *did* become a special responsibility of an assistant governor, at least until the prison welfare officer became a feature of every prison.

In the long run, however, Dr Emery's book is a study of the effects of a deliberate and rapid change in the channels, frequency, and content of communication within the complex hierarchy of a local prison, at a most important juncture in the development of the English custodial system.

Nuffield College, Oxford

N.D.W.
September 1969

Introduction

This is a report on an experiment carried out in the Bristol Local Prison over the period 1958–1960. The inmates were given greater opportunities to associate with each other in their leisure hours and an attempt was made to measure the effects of this change on the social atmosphere of the prison.

The Prison Commissioners invited the Tavistock Institute of Human Relations to participate in an experiment to test the applicability of the 'Norwich scheme' to medium-sized local prisons. This invitation was accepted on the mutual understanding that the interests of both staff and inmates would be considered and that it would probably be impossible to measure the effects of the experiment on the reform or rehabilitation of the inmates. Within this framework, detailed proposals were submitted by the Tavistock Institute and agreed upon with the Commissioners (see Appendix I). Those proposals were in large measure fulfilled in the order and manner suggested, although not in the time expected. The complexity of the situation after the introduction of the changes made it necessary to collect data up to February 1960, and the difficulty of access to information (other than records) made it necessary to spend more time and effort in the field. Relations in the prison were so sensitive that it was not possible to speed up the process by introducing research assistants.

In its completed form, the study is very much like an iceberg: the part exposed to the light of day is only a fraction of the total, and is deceptively clear and pristine. The data presented could not have been so interpreted and ordered but for the multitude of informal observations and conversations with staff and inmates. Methodologically, the key part in the study was played by the small randomly selected samples of officers and inmates. Long initial interviews with those men provided the orientation to and entrée into the daily life of the prison. Repeated interviews with the same men not only gave evidence of the psychological significance of what was going on, but also served to preserve the openness of the author's relation to the prison community. Thus, despite the considerable turnover in inmate population, it was possible to feel after a period of absence that one was returning home. Similarly, this set of relations provided the base from which one was able to explore what had, in fact, happened in disciplinary and other incidents of importance.

The samples of officers and inmates were selected with some care so that, although small, they provide a reasonably unbiased representation of what were judged to be the key groups for the purposes of this study. Amongst the uniformed staff, these are the basic grade officers who are still in the prime of their careers and, amongst the inmates, the ordinary prisoners other than those who tend to be in and out on very short sentences for such crimes as vagrancy.

Two ways in which I have used the data from these small core samples should be noted. Where a set of behavioural indices has been interpreted in a certain way, it has been assumed that this ought to be evidenced in the behaviours and attitudes of the samples. Similarly, where some general observation, e.g. about prevailing ideologies, has been invoked to explain some change, it has been assumed that this determinant ought to be evidenced in the beliefs and attitudes of the sample. In a sense, then, these core samples are called upon to serve the various functions of a microscope, trace element, and reagent. At the same time, an effort has been made to avoid basing any significant part of the argument on these data alone.

Although no conscious attempt has been made to avoid theoretical issues, this report has been overwhelmingly concerned with practical issues. It has been created under the constant awareness that statements made in it might become the basis of decisions affecting real people in the 'here and now'. This is not in itself unusual in the work of the Tavistock Institute of Human Relations. However, in this instance, I was more than ordinarily impressed with the fact that the issues involved were those of more or less suffering for the inmates and more or less danger to life and limb for the staff – they were not simply issues of more or less optimum conditions of welfare, profit, or happiness. Of still greater import was the fact that prisons, of all present-day institutions, were felt to be notoriously lacking in those higher guiding purposes and those conditions of day-to-day cooperation that normally allow a body of men to test and correct false counsel.

In so far as the report might influence decisions made for a wide class of prisons, it has been necessary to abjure those details that alone would depict Bristol Prison as a flesh-and-blood affair and to concentrate on the bare bones of oft-repeated behaviours that might tell a general story. Where speculation occurs it has, I hope, been clearly labelled as such and confined to dilemmas that have arisen in the general story – not directed to the *ifs* and *buts* of particular incidents or particular personalities. What has occurred in these years in Bristol Prison is not entirely separated from the role of certain key figures, past as well as present. The study could not have been carried out unless we had been given a clear, unambiguous guarantee that neither praise nor blame would be attributed to identifiable individuals, whether staff or inmates. Nevertheless, it is my belief that the following report would not have to be rewritten in order to accommodate details of the key individual contributions. If that state of affairs had existed, there would have been no report.

It is true, as usual, that I am deeply indebted to the people whose work and lives I have studied. It is not as easy as usual to dismiss the matter of cooperation in a few well-meaning words. There was no less cooperation *in toto* than I have found in mines, farms, schools, and factories, but the effort made, by the staff in particular, was much greater. Cooperation between social scientists and prison officials is plagued from the beginning by the common assumption that the former are, as a profession, antagonistic to prison officials and what they stand for. This is not just something believed by individual officers but, at least with the Bristol staff, had all the strength of a shared belief. Thus I was surprised in the first phase at the number of individuals wishing to be helpful, but not surprised by their unwillingness to fall out by doing so publicly, or by the amount that was done as a duty despite personal unwillingness. Naturally, a marked improvement in willing, public cooperation occurred only after the staff were convinced in practice that the research aims were concerned with their welfare as well as that of the inmates. Against this background, it is not out of place to express gratitude to the Governor, his Assistant Governor and the officers of the local branch of the Prison Officers' Association. These men, the Governor in particular, had to carry the burden of my presence around the prison over a period when it was by no means clear that my intentions were to be helpful and when there was every reason to expect me to blunderingly upset an apple-cart or two. Of the inmates, it need only be remarked that within a relation in which any question of personal gain or loss was rigorously excluded, they were – with few exceptions – cooperative. From extensive cross-checking, it is also clear that this relation encouraged in them a high degree of objectivity.

1 · Theoretical considerations of prison in general

SOCIO-PSYCHOLOGICAL ASPECTS OF PRISONS

There is in existence a small, but valuable, body of scientific literature on closed prisons as a form of social organization. Despite differences in personnel and administrative forms, there is a striking similarity in the pictures presented by those studies (a similarity that extends to the much greater body of biographical and fictionalized literature on prisons). It therefore seems reasonable to attempt an outline of the main social and psychological characteristics of closed prisons. Even if this sketch goes no further than the existing analytic studies,[1] it will serve to indicate the premises of this empirical study and thus give warning of the biases that will have unwittingly crept into it. Our observations of Bristol Prison are not discussed until the next chapter.

In examining social systems, I have elsewhere[2] found it useful to inquire into what I have termed their 'boundary conditions' – those aspects of the institutionalized complex of men and material things that mediate between the social system and the wider setting. The key and distinctive boundary condition of a productive enterprise is its technological system. Through the technological system, the enterprise achieves those productive ends that relate it to society and, also through this, there arises the major set of independent

[1] In particular, Sykes, G. *The Society of Captives,* Princeton, N.J., Princeton University Press, 1958.
Goffman, E. 'The Characteristics of Total Institutions' in *Symposium on Preventive and Social Psychiatry*, Walter Reed Army Institute of Research, Washington, 1957.
McCorkle, L. and Keon, R. 'Resocialization within Walls', *Annals,* 1954, 293, 88–98.
Grosser, G. (Ed.) *Theoretical Studies in Social Organization of the Prison,* N.Y. S.S.R.C. pamphlet 15, 1960.
[2] Emery, F. E. *Some Characteristic of Socio-Technical Systems,* mimeo. TIHR Doc. 258, 1959.

B

limitations and requirements of the social system. Hence the appropriateness of the term 'socio-technical system' for productive enterprises.

The material apparatus of a prison clearly plays no such dominant role. Unlike a factory, the typical prison problem is not that of adapting the social system to technological modifications but of trying to adapt old material means to newly modified social systems.

The key to the difference would seem to be in the obvious and indisputable fact that one is primarily concerned with things, the other with human beings. The prison achieves its institutional ends only by doing certain things with and to its inmates. It must therefore give primary consideration to the psychological properties of the inmates, because these make some measures effective and others non-effective. These common psychological properties constitute the key boundary conditions of the prison – they are an essential part of the prison and yet they must, in large measure, be treated as a 'given', i.e. as existing and obeyed laws and influences that are independent of the wishes of prison administrations. The material means (cells, walls, workshops, etc.), the type of staff, and the system of staff roles are devised, more or less appropriately, to achieve the institutional ends with the kind of inmates that are thrust upon them. Basically, the prison is one of the class of socio-psychological institutions. It differs from hospitals – medical and mental – and from religious, educational, and political institutions in that it is based on the premise of doing something against the wishes of its inmates, and usually against their interests.

If this interpretation is correct, then the key to an understanding of prisons should be the analysis of the psychological characteristics of the inmates and of the ways in which these are coped with by the staff.

The basic psychological fact about the inmates of a prison is that they are, with few exceptions, confined against their will in conditions of life not of their making and seen by them as depriving and degrading, relative to the life they would be leading if free. The generality of this state of affairs arises from the social fact that the inmates (the 'objects' handled by the institution) are defined by the State, not by any subordinate part of the society, as a morally inferior class of persons who constitute a cost to the society.

In all prison-like institutions, there is therefore to be found a body of officials concerned with confining, against their will, a much larger body of men. The staff are also impelled to maintain a detailed regulation of the internal life of the prison in order to prevent escape and carry out other institutional purposes such as maintaining health of inmates, good order, production, and rehabilitation. Even in the exceptional case, where the goal of rehabilitation is a real factor in determining the ordering of internal life, one must still expect that the great majority of the inmates will be impelled by their own needs and beliefs to seek to create a different form of life. In this persisting conflict of wills over detention and the regulation of daily life, the staff can only maintain the superiority of their own wills through their possession of greater material force. Unlike moral persuasion, the influence of physical force only extends as far as the eyes and ears of its wielders and their allies, and is only as effective as the willingness of its wielders to use it. Without exception, all classes of man-made institutions for the detention of men have been unable to achieve complete power.[1] Except where solitary confinement is the norm, an inmate society with its own ends and culture has emerged within the interstices of the official order. In the common characteristics and interaction of these two ways of life, official and inmate, it has been possible to detect social and psychological processes of conflict and accommodation that are common to all these institutions.[2] The differences arise from differences in the strength of the conflicting wills and in the resources, personal and otherwise, that are available to the contending parties. In all cases, however, these institutions continue only so long as the official order of life predominates.

The study of the common psychological characteristics of prison inmates is thus, in the first instance, a study of those forces impelling the inmates towards greater control over their own affairs at the expense of staff control. While any listing of these forces must be incomplete, the following appear to be the major ones, commonly recognized in scientific studies of prisons.

[1] Polansky, N. A. 'The Prison as an Autocracy', *J. Crim. Law & Criminology*, 1942, **33**, 16–22.
[2] See Abel, T. 'The Sociology of Concentration Camps', *Soc. Forces*, 1951, **30**, 150–154. Adler, A. G. 'Ideas Toward a Sociology of the Concentration Camps', *Amer. J. Sociol.*, 1958, **68**, 513–522. Foreman, P. B. 'Buchenwald and Modern P.O.W. Detention Policy', *Soc. Forces*, 1959, **37**, 289–298.

(a) By their usual standards of references, the inmates perceive prison as relatively depriving.

   (i) They see themselves as deprived of their normal freedom of access to pleasurable and interesting pursuits and to those things (alcohol, tobacco, gambling, and sex) that play an important role in their culture in handling intrapersonal tensions.

   (ii) They are relatively deprived of the customary supports and behavioural settings[1] for their usual living habits. In particular, they tend to find themselves with a circumscribed and impoverished 'home territory' and a lack of personal possessions.[2]

   (iii) They find themselves deprived of the usual supports for this self-image. Materially, the clothes they wear are not their own, but are simply stores issued until the next laundering; the clothes are not of their choice (although younger inmates continually seek to restyle them); they lack the supply of razor blades, brushes, cleaning materials, etc., to which normally they would have access if they wished, to maintain a reasonable level of personal appearance. Of at least equal significance, they are deprived of their usual freedom of association. Their prison associates are less likely to be acceptable as either a private or a public definition of themselves than the men and, of course, women, that they would normally seek out.

(b) By their usual standards of reference, the inmates perceive the

---

[1] There is little habitual behaviour that does not depend upon a number of supporting conditions (Tolman, E. C., *Purposive Behaviour, in Animals and Men*, New York, Century, 1932.) Because they are necessary but not sufficient conditions, and because they are familiar, they are not usually noticed – until they go wrong. In prison, a man finds that a great many of these assumed behavioural settings are absent and the initial adjustment correspondingly difficult. Empirical evidence of the role of these supports and customary behavioural settings has been advanced by Barker, R. G. & Wright, H. F. *Mid-West and its Children*, Row Peterson, 1956.

[2] Following naïve perception, scientific psychology has tended not to notice the relevance of these factors, except in animals (Hediger, *Psychology and Behaviour of Animals in Zoos and Circuses*, London, Butterworth, 1955). We side here with such diverse thinkers as Aquinas, Hegel, and Lothe, who have seen fit to remark on the necessary connection between private property and the existence of personal self-determination.

status they are accorded in prison as relatively degrading. Most inmates are accustomed to social inferiority, but find that in prison they are treated as morally inferior to officers who are socio-economically their equals and, to press home the point, that they are treated as morally no better than the other inmates (who will normally cover a wide range of criminality and depravity). The reception process for new inmates is basically conducted as a 'degradation ceremony'.[1] If this initial lesson does not sink home, the staff can usually be counted upon to contrive further informal degradation rites until the inmate accepts, at least publicly, his inferior status. In the day-to-day life of the prison, the inmate finds himself ordered about, reprimanded, and punished for the slightest misdemeanour, to a degree which is reserved in ordinary life for children and house animals.

(c) These deprivations and degradations will tend to generate in the inmate a state of emotional tension because:

    (i) They will tend to see the deprivations and degradations as unjust and unwarranted. The deprivations experienced in prison are rather more complex and varied than could be legally pronounced as punishment and, hence, easily seen as more than 'just deserts' for a crime committed; the degradations are not easily reconciled with the inmates' notion of the human dignity that the law is believed to protect. These tendencies will operate in the specific instance even when, as is usual, the inmate accepts that imprisonment and some deprivation are deserved. Whatever it is that characterizes the imprisoned criminals, it is not an absence of a sense of injustice, nor the absence of moral standards, despite the fact that in civil life they may readily commit an injustice or forget their morals. Like others, in the presence of what they consider to be injustice, the inmates will tend to experience 'that sympathetic reaction of outrage, horror, shock, resentment and anger'.[2]

[1] See Garfinkel, H. 'Conditions of Successful Degradation Ceremonies', *Amer. J. Sociol.*, 1955–6, **61**, 421–422.
[2] Cahn, E. N. *The Sense of Injustice*, New York, New York University Press, 1949.

(ii) While many of the deprivations and degradations of prison are not necessarily great in themselves (nor in themselves arouse strong or lasting feelings of injustice), they become significant because they occur so frequently, and in so many parts of prison life; the whole *prison milieu* assumes this character.[1] Even customs that are required for the inmates' own benefit acquire the connotation of alien imposed restrictions. The more these deprivations and degradations touch upon the inmate's self-image, the more the whole situation will take on this character. Where the prison milieu as a whole seems to be like this, the inmate will tend to feel tense.[2]

(iii) There is constant awareness that the deprivations and degradations are being imposed by men with whom they are in close daily contact. It is this sense of personally inflicted punishment that gives to the prison the character of 'strife' and creates its pervading atmosphere of hatred. These two features in themselves induce in the inmates many of the behaviours that they customarily show in prisons. On the one hand 'The exercise of every form of cheating and deceit occurs more readily in proportion as the situation acquires the character of strife. In such a strife, the [person] may use without hesitation, methods he would probably not employ in any but a hostile atmosphere.'[3] On the other hand, the hatred of officers, in so far as it emerges as a common feeling, provides a common denominator for joint inmate action that is otherwise lacking.[4]

In hatred, the individual is drawn away from himself, 'his weal and future'. What would be inconsistencies with respect to his own self-system may become consistent when cognition is centred upon the

[1] Lewin, K. *Dynamic Theory of Personality*, New York, McGraw-Hill, 1936, p. 129.

[2] 'The society of prisoners, however, is not only physically compressed; it is psychologically compressed' (Sykes, *ibid.*, p. 4). The psychological dynamics of a restricted space of free movement are explored in Lewin, K. & Lippitt, R. 'Field Theory and Experiment in Social Psychology', *Amer. J. Sociol.*, 1939, **44**, 868–896; **45**, 26–49.

[3] Lewin, K. *ibid.*, p. 143.

[4] Hoffer, E. *The True Believer*, London, Secker and Warburg, 1952.

hated object or person. 'Recentring' of the cognitive structure appears to be more effective, the more unified, unambiguous, vivid, and tangible the 'devil', and is more likely to take place when there already exist tendencies to hate and reject oneself. Self-rejection may in the case of the inmates derive from social rejection. Moreover, such rejection is likely to lead the object of hatred to be seen as malevolent *vis-à-vis* the person, and the existence of a malevolent and powerful human agent will lead to efforts at alliance with others.

The existence of hatred creates the psychological schism between inmates and staff that is a necessary prerequisite to the emergence and maintenance of a secret inmate world within the prison.

The above paragraphs point only to the kinds of pressure that may be expected to arise from the inmates of a closed prison. As the level of inmate pressure against the staff appears to be largely influenced by the perceived gap between life 'inside' and 'outside' (relative deprivations and degradations) it is desirable to inquire into the determinants of this perceived gap.

Three main influences can be detected:

(a) *The objective gap* between the conditions of life within and outside prison. Some gap must be expected so long as society is short of resources and imprisonment is seen as a cost that is not only unproductive but offers no certain decrease of future risks from crime. The size of the gap will depend upon the background of the different classes of prisoners sent by the courts and upon the extent to which the prison lags behind the progress or regression of external living standards. Of course, local variations will occur, as prisons differ, for instance, in the accommodation and the fare that they can offer. Further variation will also arise from the extent to which the prison can provide areas of prison life that are relatively free of the usual constraints. Thus in some long-term prisons the inmate is allowed to convert his cell into a 'home', to have a measure of free and assured interaction with inmates who can be liked and respected, and to perform work that approximates to the productive work of the outside world.

(b) *The relative potency* of the inside and outside world for the inmates. One would expect the perceived gap and the sense of deprivation and degradation to be reduced for inmates who after long imprisonment have become institutionalized. The relative potency of the standards deriving from the outside world may be lessened by losing ties to valued persons outside, becoming inured to deprivation and immune to degradation, or by attaining privileged status (official and unofficial) within the prison.

(c) *The apparent justice* with which the governor[1] and his staff enforce the prison regime. It is suggested that, in so far as justice is one of the desirable attributes of life outside, the apparent absence of justice inside would increase the inmates' awareness of the difference. This is not entirely in the hands of the governor and staff. If, for instance, the authorities treat every escape from prison as a calamity of similar magnitude (i.e. without reference to the differential risk to the community of different escapees[2]), then the governor will be under pressure to sacrifice other purposes in order to attain maximum security. This will also be true of internal incidents such as fighting between inmates. Generally, it seems that within the range of purposes pursued by a prison some, like security, are flatly opposed to the interests of the inmates; others, like good order, are consonant with, and still others, like maintenance of health and rehabilitation, supportive of their interests. A shift in policy between these various purposes could make it more or less difficult for a governor and his staff to appear to be acting justly. A further general determinant, not entirely in the governor's hands, is the defined role of the officers and their selection and training. So long as the disciplinary staff are the persons primarily responsible for enforcing the regime, the main factor preventing strife is that they should be seen to be acting as members of a class of officers, not as individuals, i.e. seen as just doing their job. Changes in selection, training, definition of duties, and even in trivial matters of dress and the like, may make it more or less difficult for officers to stay in role.

Against the above analysis of inmate tendencies and the factors influencing them, it might well be argued that the power given by the State to its prison staff is great enough to enable them to ignore the psychological characteristics of the inmates, and create any type of social system they desire. To answer this, one has to shift the focus

---

[1] I follow English usage rather than the clumsy phrase Head of the Prison although the processes apply to the latter and certainly are not peculiar to those called governors.

[2] On the judgement of risk and costs in matters involving values see 'On Chance, Loss and Risk', Ch. XV in Churchman, C. West, *Theory of Experimental Inference,* New York, Macmillan, 1948.

of analysis from the inmate, and how things seem to him, to the staff–inmate relation as it appears to the staff.

At a general level of analysis one can identify a number of forces that lessen the power of the staff:

(a) *Lack of moral power over the inmates.* It is difficult for the staff to be accepted as mentors appealing to commonly shared goals or loyalties. Even though inmates tend to feel some guilt about their crimes and accept some measure of punishment, they are unwilling to accept the degree of self-condemnation that would be implied in identifying with the staff. As a consequence, the staff must rely heavily on the exercise of physical power with all its limitations.

(b) *Lack of total surveillance of inmate life.* Total surveillance is essential to the achievement of total power based on physical force. Paradoxically, the greater the level of conflict between staff and inmates, the lesser the surveillance because of the active measures taken by the inmates to conceal their life. Use of informants ('grassing') may flourish in a period of strife, but even this is distorted by inmates to serve their conflicts and fails to provide reliable coverage.

(c) *Absence of an effective range of rewards and punishments.* The more the inmates are restricted and deprived, the less the staff can inflict punishments that will teach an appropriate lesson or offer rewards that provide an adequate incentive to inmate good behaviour. The rewards too frequently appear to the inmate as simply the absence of a deprivation. If problems of control arise, the staff are tempted to extend the range of punishments and rewards by informal means. This informal solution is not without negative effects on longer-term control.

(d) *Dependence upon the goodwill and cooperation of some inmates.* Granted that society must seek to minimize its expenditure on prisons (and subscribe to the general expectation that adults should be socially productive), it is understandable that practically all prisons in modern society are dependent upon responsible inmate labour, particularly in their domestic economy. Officers in prison posts that are not directly concerned with security will usually rely upon the cooperation of some inmates. To ensure this cooperation, they will be tempted to give informal rewards and protection. For the handling of the ordinary run of inmates, the officers will again be tempted to make a show of reasonableness in order to make it easier to move and supervise them. Recurrent difficulties because of the lack of inmate goodwill can well bring into question an officer's ability to handle men.

In parallel with these restrictions on the power of the officers are certain factors which tend to give the inmate some power *vis-à-vis* the officers:

(a) The status of the inmates is one of being only temporarily segregated. Thus, unlike a concentration camp, there is little that forces an officer to treat the inmates as non-human. As human beings with whom he is in close contact, he will find it a strain not to accord to them some of their basic rights. For instance, the staff are usually sensitive to injustices meted out to inmates by the courts, the governor, or other staff. Beyond this are the special problems raised by the fact that many inmates are recognized by the staff to have in civil life a status similar or even superior to their own. Deference, in the latter case, is not unknown.

(b) As human beings, the inmates have intentions, memories, and anticipations. The staff learn early in their careers that exercise of their powers may not only give an inmate pain or pleasure but elicit a planned course of counteraction. Among themselves, the staff recount the more striking instances where a grudge against an officer has been settled by an inmate, by proxy or by informing to the higher authorities.

(c) The inmates are frequently able to establish personal relations that are satisfying to an officer. Despite the obvious difficulties, there is always at any one time in a prison a network of personal relations between some officers and some inmates. Many of these will be convivial, and some rather uneasy friendships. In part, this is due to general cultural and personal factors; but, in part, it seems due to the lack of personalized supports that the disciplinary officer finds in his role. My own contact with the staff of a single prison suggests that this job tends to alienate its holder from the sympathetic support of outsiders, even his spouse; and, within the prison, it is difficult to display to other staff members the need for personal support. It is a constant temptation for many to seek some human understanding of their problems from inmates who know something of the prison world in which the problems arise and seem grateful for a little reciprocal understanding.

To trace further this general process, it is necessary to examine the dilemmas in the role of the disciplinary officer and its relation to that of the governor.

ROLE DILEMMAS IN A CLOSED PRISON

Where men are confined under conditions giving rise to considerable tension, it is unlikely that they will, of their own accord, develop or maintain the normally acceptable standards of individual and community behaviour. Although the inmates share to some extent in a common fate, this is only temporary. Many of them are in prison because of psychopathic tendencies; most are not interdependent with respect to achievement of any primary work-task. The usual bases for cooperative living are absent, and hence, without actively exerted restraining forces, one could expect such a prison community to achieve stability only at a level where organized gangs of inmates could more or less freely exploit and manipulate other inmates and where the gangs had fairly free access to the outside world through corrupted members of the staff. The limits to these processes would be set, for both the dominant inmates and the corrupted elements on such a staff, by the danger of bringing about the intervention of social forces from without the prison. (There is a substantial body of empirical evidence on the existence of these tendencies in prisons, concentration camps, and other institutions where large groups of persons are held under conditions of deprivation without some common binding force of political or religious beliefs or military *esprit de corps. Vide* Abel, fn 2, p. 3 above.)

Certain of the measures customarily taken to limit this natural tendency towards inmate self-government are of reasonable effectiveness; others bring about certain improvements in immediate control, but in the long run paradoxically increase the difficulties of control because they raise the general level of tension in the prison and render it more difficult for the governor to control and direct his staff, to know his inmates, or to dispense justice.

Among the effective measures are those that enhance and support a uniformly defined and non-contradictory status difference between the staff and the inmates, and those that reduce the element of personal judgement and personal involvement in matters of control. Together, these measures define the relation between staff and inmates as a generalized one of dominance of one kind of person over another.

It seems clear, in general terms, that the stronger the tendency in a particular prison toward 'semi-official inmate government', the greater the need for the staff to have means for maintaining an adequate social distance between themselves and the inmates. The difference in the appearance and quality of the uniforms, the one-sided possession of keys and weapons, and the forms and manner of personal address are a clear and constant reminder to all that two classes of differently privileged persons, not just individuals, confront each other. Rules restricting informal conversations with inmates and private contact with their relatives and friends outside help to protect the staff member from bribery, from trickery, and from conflicts between his personal sympathies and his duties.

Detailed orders about the conduct of every aspect of prison routine, rules to cover all possible inmate acts of non-compliance, and the separation of the functions of apprehension and judgement, all help the officer to use his authority impersonally.

These status devices and rules provide the officer with a definition of his role *vis-à-vis* the inmates. The definition is a secure basis for individual and joint staff action, providing that the rules are enforceable, that the officer has at his disposal a range of incentives and punishments adequate for inducing compliance in all his changes, and that they can be regarded as representing the standpoint of the third party which is the penultimate source of authority within the prison system. All that a man needs as a prison officer, given a secure role definition, is a set of convictions about the inmates such that for every class of probable inmate behaviours he has a corresponding class of reactions.[1] Where these three conditions are present – clear unambiguous role definition, secure supports for the role, and typing of the role behaviours of the inmates – there is much less danger of the staff allowing their role to be significantly influenced in give-and-take with the inmates or of prison standards being accommodated to inmate pressures.

[1] cf. Steiner, I. D. 'Interpersonal Behaviour as Influenced by Accuracy of Social Perception', *Psychol. Rev.*, 1955, **62**, 268–274.

While these common measures are reasonably effective, there are grounds for believing that the definition of role, and the way it is learnt, contain the germ of some of the persistent difficulties observed in it. The role of prison officer is only meaningful in its relation to the complementary role of prison inmate. Hence, as already stated, it can be operated only by having some more or less appropriate picture of the inmates. In any contact with the inmates, an officer actually sees a particular individual or group of individuals in a concrete situation; before he can respond according to his defined role, he must interpret what he sees. This interpretation may stem from projection[1] – e.g. thinking he knows what X is like, the officer may conclude that 'X is trying to do Y' – or it may stem from past experience – e.g. 'This looks like the old business of Y'. One would hope that 'projection' would be based on past experience; in practice, contrasting modes of interpretation tend to arise as projection tends to be based on incorrect or inadequate assumptions about others.[2] From the speed with which officers claimed they first adjusted to the prison situation (usually about two weeks for the Bristol sample), it looks very much as if their basic beliefs about inmates are stereotypes taken over from other staff, not knowledge created by their own interactions with prisoners. These stereotypes are all negative, some more so than others.

For several reasons this early predominance of projective interpretation is likely to persist. First, the factors that usually limit or overcome this tendency in an ordinary social system are absent. Thus, except for prisons with long-term inmates, the persons occupying the roles of inmate *vis-à-vis* the officer are continually changing, and it is difficult for any alternative or deeper conception of the role to emerge. It will, for instance, be harder for the new officer to learn that variations in role behaviour may, because of differences in personality, be functionally equivalent so far as the social system is

[1] 'Projection' is here used only to refer to projection into observed behaviour of prior assumptions about the actor, i.e. to *argument ad hominem*. This usage and most of the argument follows Turner, R. H. 'Role Taking, Role Standpoint and Reference Group Behaviour', *Amer. J. Sociol.*, 1955–6, **61**, 316–328. For an analysis of the importance of this mode of interpretation in everyday thinking, see also Heider F. *The Psychology of Interpersonal Relations,* New York, Wiley, 1958.
[2] Ichheiser, G. 'Misunderstandings in Human Relations', *Amer. J. Sociol.*, 1949, **55**, part 2.

concerned. The most effective means of overcoming projective tendencies, namely, rotation between complementary roles, is completely excluded by the circumstances.

The officer cannot even temporarily take on the role of inmate and expect to be returned to his previous role. The inmate, for equally sound reasons, is rigorously excluded from ever being selected into the service. Nevertheless, although a practical impossibility, it should be noted that lack of role exchange creates a major obstacle to an officer's going beyond his current stereotypes to an understanding of his own role and of the total social system to which these roles belong. Second, in so far as the power to define the situation rests primarily in the hands of the staff,[1] their definitions of the situation will tend to be self-justifying. The inmate will tend to find life easier if he accepts these definitions as an objective part of his social environment. With long exposure to the officers and with the loss of alternative standards of reference, he will even start to accept as his own the value judgements underlying these definitions. Because this tends to be the result of staff dominance, the above-mentioned effect of extended experience with the same persons in the same roles (as in long-term prisons) will not necessarily deepen insight into those roles. The major effect will be to create a greater sensitiveness to situational indications of inmate behaviour and hence, while making the officers better supervisors, lessen the need to watch or understand the individual *per se*.

This reliance on stereotyped beliefs has several consequences. It helps the officers to preserve a considerable social distance between themselves and the inmates. Provided the level of tension in the prison is high enough to make staff–inmate friendliness dangerous, it could be said that the best test of whether a new man will make a good officer is whether he dons the stereotypes as readily as he dons his uniform. The reliance on negative stereotypes also helps to keep the officer in the tense prison from personal involvement with the fate of the inmates and hence to avoid the painful and institutionally inefficient responses of sympathy, pity, shame, or guilt that would be evoked by his doing or seeing the same things done to ordinary people in his ordinary social world. However, the handling of inmates

[1] They do not, of course, have a monopoly of power. They learn early in their careers that inmates can, at a cost to themselves, exercise serious sanctions against an individual officer.

on the basis of negative stereotypes is a fertile source of misunder-standings. Where, as a result, blame and punishment are wrongly attributed or wrongly proportioned, the inmate will see it as injustice and will not be inclined to excuse it on the grounds that the staff cannot help their prejudices. These misunderstandings at the expense of the inmate may thus set going the sort of process that one suspects is always latent in a complementary role pattern where one role is to be dominant and depriving. The matter becomes more serious in a prison because, if the inmate does attribute the perceived injustice to hatred of himself, he is not able to protect himself from the threat by moving out of the situation. He is, therefore, likely to hate the officer in turn, or go in constant fear of him, and further enforced contact with the officer will lead to an increasing convergence of their behaviours. This both resembles and contrasts with a love-relation; if the inmate allows his anger and hatred to become foremost, he provides the officer with living justification for the way he interprets his role and, at the same time, the hatred of the officer tends to become the psychological world of the inmate. The manner in which both parties goad each other makes the phenomena look like pathological sado-masochism. While latent sadistic tendencies would undoubtedly heighten the chances of a particular officer's becom-ing involved in this way, I am suggesting that the same effect can arise from conscientious carrying out of the officer role in a tense prison.[1]

Thus, in itself, the role of prison officer is likely to be a source of frequent but generally minor conflicts. If the prison is tense, there will be a greater pressure to rely on the stereotypes and a greater willingness to develop some staff–inmate conflicts to the point where the inmate is literally persecuted. Also, the efficacy and self-justifying nature of these stereotypes make it much more difficult for the staff to accept that any change in the make-up of the prison population or in the aims of the prison system can justify a change in their role.

So far we have dealt with difficulties arising from the definition of the officer role and the perceptions of the complementary role of the inmate. Also difficulties may arise from changes in the way the staff see their role supported and their beliefs shared by the third party –

[1] The obvious implication is that, in a less tense prison, the officers concerned would cease to engage in activities of this sort. At Bristol, this happened, and the change of heart was observed by the inmates.

the governor – and, less immediately the heads of the Prison Service.

These difficulties centre upon the administration of justice. This is not a straightforward matter in a prison and needs to be briefly considered before analysing the particular difficulties that arise between officers and the governor.[1]

Normally, punishment is for the crime not the person. To administer this, it is desirable (a) that those punishing should not have to live with the criminal (unless, as in certain primitive tribes, it is communally administered) and, (b) as a further safeguard, the same people should not both apprehend and punish. In prison, these requirements are partly met by the division between the roles of governor and of uniformed staff. As chief executive officer, he must have their cooperation, and for this he must be prepared to pay the price of seeing their problems from their point of view. No matter how much he tries to avoid bias in this respect, he must also attend to the fact that the inmate before him for punishment is a man with a history and a future in *his* prison community. The inmate must be taught that he cannot win in a fight against the staff. Similarly, the inmates at large must be taught that certain kinds of action will not be tolerated. The administration of justice in a prison should teach these lessons or, as staff and inmates put it, 'draw the lines'. However, the tempering of justice for administrative ends increases the likelihood that the inmates will feel that they are as a rule denied justice unless, of course, the administrative ends are thought to be justifiable.

Within this setting, there is a formal division of labour between governor and officers in the matter of discipline: the latter apprehend and the former adjudicates. Undoubtedly, the task of the officers is made easier in the long run if there is a real difference, one that is perceivable to the inmates, between apprehension and punishment. This distinction lessens the likelihood that an officer will become or will be seen as a source of injustice and hence lessens the build-up of inmate hostilities against him, because the inmates can more readily accept that the officer is only doing his duty in reporting any observed misdemeanour. It is up to the governor in his role of judge to sort out

[1] In the United Kingdom, legal justice, *per se*, is the province of the courts not the prison administration. It is not possible, however, to consider prison life without taking account of the sense of injustice that can arise from enforcement of administrative regulations.

the pros and cons. The restrictions that the officer has to enforce are complex and related to the main tasks of good order and security. However, if the officer perceives that they are so related and if he accepts that detection and punishment of violations have an important educational function for the prison as a whole, then it is certainly easier for an officer to report an inmate on the grounds of what appears to be the case without feeling that he is expected by the inmate or governor to make his own judgement of guilt and appropriate punishment on the basis of various contingencies and possibilities. For example, to give an actual incident, an inmate throws water from a landing over an officer standing below. The officer has seen enough of what led up to it to believe that it was accidental. What, however, happens if he has to make judgement is that the man must nevertheless be punished because, accident or not, it occurred publicly and may be seen by some of the other inmates as a blow struck in their cause or by nearby officers as a sign of weakness on his part. In this case, it is quite likely that the inmate concerned and other inmates observing the event will think it personal spite. On the other hand, if the officer takes the incident before the governor, he can report the prisoner under rule 'X' (general misbehaviour) instead of rule 'Y' (aggression toward an officer) and state, 'I do believe that he did not intend it.' The governor can, for reasons acceptable to the inmate, inflict a minor punishment. The separation of apprehension and judgement enables this incident to serve its educational function and yet be sealed off so that there is no carry-over of ill feelings.

It is not easy to maintain this separation. There is the natural tendency for the officer-on-the-spot to feel that he understands more of what is going on than does the distant judge; neither the limitations of his perception nor the long-range value for him of the separation of functions are as obvious and as convincing as what he thinks he sees in front of him. This general tendency is not enough to explain the difficulties encountered in maintaining the independent adjudicating function. If conditions in prison were like those of industrial organizations, steps could be taken to ensure that the governor and his deputy had sufficient knowledge of the staff roles and the daily life of their prison to make judgements that were patently realistic. However, with the high level of tension existing in prison, the informal and personal nature of staff–inmate hostilities will increase the disparity between what is known to the officer and what is or can be

c

known to the governor. The staff, in seeking to get on top of the trouble, will find themselves involved in a great many personal struggles with particularly fractious inmates and groups of inmates. The officer-on-the-spot then knows that he knows more than his governor (certainly more than his governor can officially admit to knowing) because he has taken steps to conceal certain informal practices of his own and will not willingly admit to having insufficient discipline and respect from his charges. In these circumstances, the staff effectively arrogate to themselves part of the governor's adjudicating function, and it becomes increasingly difficult for the governor to be aware of the significance of even a simple report. Thus an officer, in reporting a prisoner for a relatively minor instance of insubordination, may be quite sure in his mind that this is just one further show of defiance by a particular clique; or that it is the first time he has been able to 'get something on' a particularly obnoxious or cunning trouble-maker; or that it is one more milestone in a running battle between himself and the particular inmate. These things will be very real to the officers, and the governor will be under strong pressure from them to 'back them up', i.e. to accept that if they put an inmate on report, there are good reasons for it, even if these reasons cannot be fully disclosed or formally proved. The staff demand in effect that, in a state of tension, the governor should resign some of his authority and declare a state of martial law. Where these conditions prevail, the governor may likewise find it difficult to work with external controlling bodies, to convey to them, for instance, why two men before them for inflicting bodily harm should both receive severe punishment, although one was clearly the aggressor and the harm done was negligible. Formal controls, such as the English ones of Visiting Magistrate and Visiting Committee, are both likely to be ineffective when the staff and inmates are involved in something like guerrilla warfare. They will find it difficult to do justice and more difficult to be seen as doing justice. If the Visiting Committee sense and follow the inclinations of the governor in making their judgement, they in fact abrogate their independent role. If they insist on their independent role, they may well find themselves with insufficient knowledge of the cases under consideration.

This freezing-up under tension of the formal system of checks and balances on the staff's handling of the inmates, is only a matter of degree. At each point, principal officer, chief officer, governor,

Visiting Committee,[1] there is a measure of genuine independence and a corresponding set of limits to the extent to which they can or will allow their function to be taken over by others. Even when the uniformed staff are apparently being 'backed up to the hilt, all along the line' (this being one old officer's description of the ideal), they are still aware of these tacit limits and, furthermore, become relatively more anxious about inmates' invoking the unofficial controls of public opinion, such as questions in the legislature and the press.

Thus, while a particular governor may, for personal reasons, default in his role as judge and thus contribute to a deterioration in staff–inmate relations, it is more likely that a governor will find it difficult to operate this part of his role because, for other reasons, staff–inmate relations have deteriorated. The manner in which formal controls break down may usefully be examined a little further in order to disclose more fully the instability of the conventional prison setting and the relative powerlessness of good intentions to restore the situation.

It has been noted that, in a period of rising tension, it is difficult for a governor to do other than back the staff. If he follows this, the easier, course, the situation does not automatically right itself. Personal vendettas will build up all the more easily because the governor in backing the staff will have resigned the function that he alone can perform – relating judgement and punishment to the requirements of the prison as a whole. Thus, when he is fulfilling his role of judge, the governor is normally passing judgement upon both the officer and the inmate. This, which only occasionally occurs in a court of law, is the usual thing in the prison because the officer and inmate have to go on living with each other. The absence of any formal judgement on the officer does not alter this fact – as can readily be discovered by listening to officers discussing with each other the way their cases have been handled. The daily hearings are undoubtedly the most significant contact the governor has with the staff and inmates, since it is here that both parties get the clearest indications of how the governor wants the prison run. It is also for the inmates the key indicator of governor–staff relations. In the absence of the broader perspective, it is very difficult for staff to judge a case on other than those things that come within their orbit of experience and responsibility. Both staff and governor would have

[1] This list does not exhaust the range of formal controls in English prisons.

plenty of incidents to justify their firm line. As one of the effects of heightened tension is to create scapegoating and factionalism, they would also be provided with the reason for increasing strife, namely the outbreak of hostilities between groups of locals versus Londoners, one draft against another, Irish against Protestants, etc.

For this and the more obvious reasons mentioned earlier, the practical fusion of apprehension and judgement will tend to increase the inmate feeling of being unjustly persecuted and harassed by the staff and hence lead to even more conflict. A higher level of tension could be expected to occur among inmates as well as between inmates and staff. As daily life becomes more fraught with danger for the inmates, persecutory delusions and suspicions of 'grassing' can be expected to flourish; the more timid will withdraw into their shells 'to do their own bird' and, by the same token, will be easier targets for the predatory cliques.

This is but one further aspect of what has earlier been described as the inherently unstable character of the conventional prison system. When the balance shifts, the ordinary stabilizing devices fail, and what emerges (in this case the apparent identity of apprehension and judgement) tends to increase the shift.

2 · Basic characteristics of Bristol Prison

While there are good reasons for attending to social and psychological processes common to all prisons, it is also a necessary caution to define a narrower empirical class of prisons that are more obviously similar to Bristol and hence to which the findings of this study may more readily be extended. It is also necessary to describe the concrete features of Bristol Prison, since they provide the setting for the processes being studied.

Bristol Prison is a Local Prison with an average population, during 1957–1960, of approximately 360 men and boys.

Of the total time served in English and Welsh prisons, about three-quarters is served in Local Prisons, with the rest about equally divided between Central and Regional Prisons. As the latter handle long-term prisoners, the Locals have to handle more than 90 per cent of all the men who go to prison in any one year. The problems of the Local Prison are thus of considerable importance within the prison system of England and Wales. However, although all the Local Prisons operate within the same system, under the same regulations, with much the same buildings and work programmes, and with considerable interchange of staff, there are noticeable differences in their social atmospheres, apparently due to differences in size. The smaller Locals are generally seen by those staff and inmates who have experienced all sizes as more intimate and 'cosy' and the larger ones as more impersonal, officious, 'Yankee-style' prisons; the medium-sized vary considerably between these extremes. The twenty-five Local Prisons in 1957 ranged in size of average daily population from 110 to 1,238. Bristol is one of the six medium-sized Local Prisons that has a daily average of between 300 and 500 inmates. Altogether, the medium-sized Locals hold approximately 2,600 inmates (usually between 15 to 20 per cent of the total prison population).

The only striking difference between Bristol and the other medium-sized Locals is its higher incidence of reported inmate offences. In fact, for the four years prior to 1958, Bristol Prison had a rate of offences higher than any other Local irrespective of size. This difference suggests a persistently higher level of tension between staff and inmates, but the difference is not so great as to warrant any *a priori* assumption of qualitative difference.

The claim that this difference does not represent a significant and persistent qualitative difference is important if the findings in Bristol are to be generalized. Hence it is necessary to consider certain additional pertinent facts. While Bristol has a consistently higher incidence of offences over the four-year period, there were two years in which another Local had a similar incidence. Furthermore, if one examines the relative seriousness of the reported offences, it is apparent that Bristol, while higher in this respect, was not markedly so. The order of magnitude of the differences shown in *Table 1* does not suggest anything more than a difference in degree; namely, that one

Table 1 – Percentage of all offences that are 'serious'*

	Bristol	Mean for all local prisons
1954	50	45
1955	55	46
1956	46	49
1957	47	45

* By 'serious' is meant acts of 'violence, damage to property, and insubordination', i.e. offences that are most likely to carry a connotation of attack on authority.

could expect to find Bristol to be like other prisons, only 'screwed down' more. It should, because of this, provide a clearer picture of the social and psychological processes involved in controlling and managing a Local Prison.

CONCRETE FEATURES OF BRISTOL PRISON

Physical Setting
Bristol Prison is located in a closely-settled housing area. It is surrounded by a twenty-foot brick wall penetrated by only one solid gate. Within the walls are two large brick buildings and a series of

smaller ancillary buildings, some used for inmates to meet their visitors, for classes, and for reception and discharge of inmates; others used as officers' mess, kitchen, stores, hospital, baths, wood-shed, and workshops. The larger of the two brick buildings houses administrative offices, the chapel, and the main cell block, 'A' Hall. The other large building is for practical purposes a wing of the main block and houses the library, the prison psychologist, and the smaller cell block, 'D' Hall. Covered passageways connect 'D' Hall, the class-rooms, hospital, and main workshop to 'A' Hall. Like the cell blocks in most other Locals, 'A' Hall was built to provide the maximum number of secure, one-man cells, the minimum allow-ance of space for the movement of men to and from the cells, and fullest possible observation of cell doorways, passageways, and stairs from a central position. The cells are evenly distributed on four landings, with the top three landings served by catwalks and connected by a steep, narrow, central staircase. A glass ceiling provides adequate light in daytime. 'D' Hall is similarly constructed but, having fewer landings, has more floor space per inmate.

From the staff viewpoint, the compactness of the main cell blocks facilitates control over certain routine matters, but the scatter of ancillary buildings and workshops creates difficulties for controlling movement, and the staff is continuously harassed by the overall lack of 'secure' space for almost all the needs of the prison, including sleeping. As many as one-third of the cells have to be used for sleeping three prisoners instead of the one for which they were designed.[1] There is no lack of relatively 'insecure' space in the yards of the prison, but, apart from the exercise rings and thoroughfares, it is not seen by the staff as useful for their purposes. The physical setting thus makes it difficult for the staff to handle the inmates other than *en masse* or as administrative integers to be switched from cell to cell or from one work-place to another as the pressure of numbers requires. The setting provided a high degree of security for the old system of individual confinement and work in the cells, but does not do so for the present-day system. On the contrary, it seems to demand of the staff greater conscious attention to security.

For the inmates, there is overcrowding in the cells (or constant risk of it unless they are homosexual or awaiting trial), overcrowding at

[1] The allocation of two prisoners to a cell is ruled out because of the problems it creates.

the recesses for 'slopping-out'[1] and on the landings during movement, overcrowding in the main workshops, and overcrowding in the exercise ring. These afore-mentioned parts of the physical structure are the only parts with which the average inmate is in regular daily contact. Hence, it is fair to state that overcrowding is for the inmates a primary characteristic of the Local Prison. They must, because of the setting, expect to be more or less continuously exposed to and forced to rub shoulders with strangers, many of them violent and treacherous. They will find it very difficult to achieve any degree of privacy or to associate selectively with inmates of their own choosing. In none of these physical respects does the Bristol Prison present a setting for staff and inmates that is very different from other Local Prisons. Just as 'D' Hall has more space per inmate than 'A' Hall, and thus allows greater differentiation in management procedures, so do some Locals have more space than Bristol. None, however, would seem to have sufficient space to allow for a range of low- to high-security areas that would match the varying requirements of their inmate populations or permit most handling to be done in small groups of manageable size.

The Inmate Population

Persons come into Bristol Prison for all kinds of crimes. The majority come in for theft, burglary, and similar crimes against property, but there is always a substantial minority who have been imprisoned for fraud, violence, or sexual offences. Some idea of the relative frequency of these is given in *Table 2*:

Table 2 – Percentage distribution of crimes leading
to imprisonment at Bristol*

	1957	1958
Larceny & breaking	55	53
Fraud, etc.	9	9
Violence	12	12
Heterosexual	7	8
Homosexual	4	3
Other	13	15
	(458 = 100%)	(481 = 100%)

* For both years the data are based on samples of entrants.

[1] Emptying-out the overnight toilet buckets.

For the most part, these differences in reasons for imprisonment do not make much difference in the daily life of the prison. Those imprisoned for fraud and related 'white-collar' crimes tend to be better-educated, more intelligent, and more frequently of middle-class status. Such men tend to be sought after by the staff for the 'red-band' or 'trusties' roles. Not only are their abilities more appropriate for these jobs, but their desire to remain aloof from the other inmates makes them less likely to abuse a trust on their behalf. Homosexuals have to be kept in single cells, but otherwise are not normally troublesome to staff or inmates. Sexual offenders against children tend to be shunned by staff and inmates alike, but do not for this particular reason become a predictable source of trouble. Those imprisoned for violence are not necessarily the ones most likely to attack the staff, although they may be drawn into the service of those running the illegal gambling and trading. Thus, the problems posed by differences in reasons for imprisonment seem to be diverse but minor. (This is not true of all such differences. Major problems arise if a substantial number of inmates in a prison are there for non-criminal reasons, e.g. politics or conscientious objection to military service.)

While the level of education and intelligence seems to be below the average for comparable age-groups of the population at large (of the 939 cases referred to in the above table, approximately half were below the 25th percentile of the population for performance on the Raven's Matrices Test of Intelligence), only a small proportion is too dull to cooperate. These few tend to be disruptive in that they are readily victimized by other inmates or used as unwitting tools against staff.

More important for the character of the prison than the reasons for imprisonment are the differences in length of sentence and previous prison experience.

Regardless of crime committed, the Local Prisons hold all ordinary prisoners (i.e. recidivists) with sentences of less than five years, and they act as clearing-houses or temporary holding-places for all other classes of prisoner. Ordinary prisoners with sentences of more than five years spend up to the first twenty months in a Local. That Bristol is no different in this respect can be seen from *Table 3*.

These diverse classifications carry different implications for the rate of turnover – those listed under 'D' Hall staying for shorter periods than those in 'A' Hall. The classifications also pose problems of day-to-day management since the Borstal Trainees, the Young Prisoners, the Adult Stars, the Civil Prisoners, and the Remand Prisoners all have to be segregated from ordinaries and several of the groups from each other. Under the overcrowded conditions described above, this is a considerable drain on administrative resources.

Table 3 – Average composition of Bristol Prison population, October 1957 – February 1960

'A' Hall		'D' Hall	
Corrective training and Preventive detention and Long-term Ordinaries	10	Borstal Trainees and Young Prisoners	6
		Stars,* Civil, Remand	17
Short-term Ordinaries (under four years)	67		
	77%		23%
	(100% = 366 inmates)		

* First offenders.

The usual solution, which is followed at Bristol, is to create what are practically two prisons within the same outer wall, sharing services such as kitchen, hospital, stores, reception, and office administration, but with no overlap of inmate populations and only a restricted interchange of staff. Each sub-system tends to have its own characteristics and to be more comparable to its equivalent in other Local Prisons than to the other. Compared with 'A' Hall, 'D' Hall has a younger population, less experienced in the ways of prison life and, expecting only a short stay, less concerned with settling down in Bristol Prison. While the Borstal Trainees and Young Prisoners tend to be an emotionally volatile group, their lack of prison experience and rapid turnover mitigates against the formation of a resistant inmate society. Similarly, while the Remand and Civil Prisoners usually include some men with previous prison experience, these are few in number, pretty well segregated, and in any case so concerned with their own trial or their special privileges that they present few problems of control. The problems of controlling 'D' Hall only begin to approach those of 'A' Hall when there is a hold-up in transfers, and a body of Borstal Trainees and Young Prisoners or Stars has to be held for a period of months.

In terms of both numbers and length of stay, 'A' Hall is the core of the Local Prison. Turnover, while very much lower than in 'D' Hall, is still an administrative problem, since at any time about half the population is serving sentences of eight months or less. Over a period of six months, about forty per cent of the original population can be expected to leave and their beds and work-places to be occupied by new inmates. This turnover inhibits the growth of an inmate society, but it does so rather less than would be expected of, say, a military unit with similar turnover. The Local Prison draws most of its inmates from the surrounding localities and, invariably, draws very heavily on one or two not-so-select suburbs of the major city in its catchment-area. Hence, many of its inmates come from the same area, and know each other or have common acquaintances. Repeated and overlapping periods of imprisonment also help to maintain a core of stable inmate relations. Of at least equal importance to these personal networks is the continuity of inmate culture. The ease with which the inmate culture is transmitted over time is, for the most part, due to its basic values being derived, even if in a distorted way, from the values prevalent in the working classes of the society. This culture is primarily oriented to coping with and exploiting the weakness of the individual staff, the more stable system of staff roles and rules, and the familiar environmental features of the prison. Unlike most cultures, the inmate culture does not arise from evaluations of men who are freely engaged in common endeavours, and consequently it does not define the characteristics and potentialities of the inmate group beyond a crude typing of inmate and staff roles and a cultural definition of inmate suffering and its conditions (i.e. ways of 'doing bird'). It is a culture without heroes or villains because there are no 'Common Causes'. The features to which the inmate culture refer are fairly similar in all Local Prisons, and hence one can understand why Ordinaries, having had previous experience in another prison, are able so quickly to assimilate the local variations and relate themselves in a meaningful way to the pattern of inmate life.

The age composition of 'A' Hall differs considerably from that of 'D' Hall.

Figure 1 Age composition of 'A' Hall
(Average of three measures at six-month intervals)

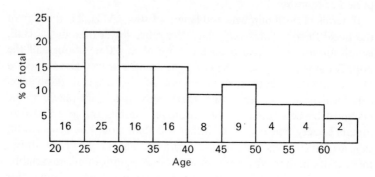

'A' Hall is largely populated by physically fit men, about sixty per cent being between twenty-five and forty years of age, but there are two constant minorities: one of about fifteen per cent, of men over fifty, chronically ill or physically handicapped; and the other, of similar proportion, of young men under twenty-five. The over-forties are a very settled group with a rate of inmate offences equal to only about one-fourth of the average, but among them are many who confront the staff with the sort of problems to be found in old men's homes. The under-twenty-fives form a marked contrast, with their sensitivity to any suggestion of being 'pushed around' and their concern with proving their 'manliness'. Unlike the Young Prisoners of 'D' Hall, they are under pressure to relate themselves to the inmate culture and, consequently, their offences are more frequently serious. This minority tends to offend at twice the average rate for 'A' Hall.

Thus, while relatively homogeneous with respect to classification, 'A' Hall shows major differences according to age. It is believed that the age differential is the most significant of the ecological variables affecting the life of the inmates and staff control. Previous crime shows no major relation, and differences in prison experience tend to be related to age.

The Staff

Overall responsibility for the Bristol Prison is vested in the governor and shared with his deputy. This responsibility is primarily exercised through the basic-grade officers. Additional uniformed officers are in charge of work and hospital activities. The following table shows the distribution at the end of August 1958. Although the actual numbers in the different categories are subject to change with changes in work-load, these figures represent a pattern of staffing common to this type of prison.

On the senior staff are a senior medical officer, the steward, and a psychologist. In addition, there are civilian staff handling administrative and other duties requiring little or no contact with the inmates.

Table 4 – Composition of the uniformed staff, August 1958

| Disciplinary staff | Ancillary staff | |
	Works	Hospital
Chief officers I & II	Cook	Hospital PO
4 Principal officers	2 Engineers	6 Hospital officers
34 Officers	5 Instructors	
	6 Trade assistants	

The main fact emerging from *Table 4* is the small number of disciplinary staff available to handle the inmates. The ratio of 1 to 10 given by a direct comparison of the numbers is far greater than what occurs in practice. Thus, even for those times of the day when trouble is likely to occur – on exercise and in the shops – the ratio is more likely to be one officer to thirty inmates. The reasons for this are not hard to uncover. Whereas the inmates are present for twenty-four hours a day, seven days a week, the staff has to be given a forty-two-hour week. Considerable splitting of shifts has to be done even to cover the period from 7 a.m. to 5 p.m. In addition, a number of special posts have to be filled from the ranks of the officers (gate-keeper, chief officer's clerk, mail censor, librarian, prisoners' canteen officer, bath house officer, reception); special duties have to be carried out (courts, escorts, and supervising visits); the division of the prison into 'A' Hall and 'D' Hall, while it eases the problems of control and lessens the dangers of contamination, also creates some duplication of work; and lastly, there is a continual loss due to sickness and annual leave (equivalent to the loss of 4–6 men for a staff this size).

To maintain security and order under these conditions, there has developed a system that aims to keep the men securely locked in their cells for as long as is commensurate with the exercise, work, educational, religious, and other activities that are laid down by the Commissioners or governor. A system of alarms enables reinforcements of staff to be brought rapidly to any point where trouble breaks out, or is threatened, and a routine of counting, searching, and supervising ensures that as much as possible of the inmates' behaviour is under constant observation.

How effectively the staff carries out these duties is, in part, dependent upon their age and experience. *Table 5* shows that at 1 August 1958 none of the officers was under thirty years of age.

Table 5 – Age distribution of officers (1 August 1958)

Years of age	Ordinary officers	Works & hospital	Chiefs & POs
30–39	20	5	—
40–49	8	9	2
50+	7	5	7

On the average, the ordinary officers are older than the inmates, although this one difference is obvious only when they are dealing with the inmates under twenty-five years of age. All the officers are of an age at which they can be expected to be fairly self-assured about their maturity, and the majority of the ordinary officers are still short of the age at which they might be expected to take things a little easier. Furthermore, most of them entered the service in their twenties or early thirties, so they have accumulated some years of experience in the job and can be expected to be confident in their ability to handle it.

Table 6 – Length of service of basic-grade staff
(August 1958)

		Ordinary officers	Works & hospital
	13+ yrs.	5	6
Joining	5–12	25	11
post-war	under 5	5	2

In addition, two-thirds of the ordinary officers have spent at least the past five years in Bristol, and fifteen have spent nine or more years. This period is sufficiently long for the staff, individually, to have a detailed and valid picture of the setting and the people with whom they have to work. It is also long enough for a stable, closely masked, informal social structure to emerge between the staff. However, this does not appear to have occured, even though their jobs are interdependent, in the sense that one officer's laxity threatens the safety of others and one officer's laziness increases the work of others. Parallel to what is observed among the inmates, there are several small cliques, some pair relations, and a number of isolates. It is as if the strains of the job and the modes of adjustment are so predominantly personal that there is a reluctance to develop relations even of reciprocated dependence on others.

It is unlikely that persistent difficulties in administration or in staff–inmate relations could be traced to staff inexperience. Such difficulties are more likely to arise from factors inherent in the established system of staff–inmate roles and the kinds of people who fill them. These are the factors that are most common to different local prisons. The governor, assistant governor, chief, and principal officers are brought in from other prisons, and the basic-grade officers have had sufficient experience of other prisons to ensure that staff roles at Bristol are defined in ways that are common to other Local Prisons. Approximately one-third of the basic-grade officers have served more than three years in a Central Prison, and the rest have served 'detached duties' of more than a month each at several other prisons. Thus any difficulties that may be found in examination of staff roles at Bristol are likely also to be found in other Locals.

This does not mean, however, that the way in which staff roles are carried out is entirely determined by formal definition. The precepts of the senior staff, common practice, and the individual officer's interpretation of his own experience are likely to carry in them some reflection of the values, standards, and external commitments that the officers bring with them to the job. Although there is no detailed evidence on the Prison Service at large, there are grounds for suspecting that the Bristol staff reasonably represents the nature of these values, standards, and external commitments. From personal interviews with twenty of the thirty-four ordinary officers, it is possible to reconstruct the following as the model pattern of life experiences before entering the prison service:

- brought up in a working-class family (only two officers were from lower middle-class families);
- left school at fourteen years of age (but of those born after 1920, half had one or two further years of study. Only two attended grammar school);
- first steady job most likely to have been in unskilled or semi-skilled labouring (least likely to be in white-collar work);
- military service with non-commissioned rank (for the majority, this was wartime service);
- married with children;
- post-war employment in unskilled or semi-skilled labouring;
- dissatisfaction with factory or mill work and primary concern with lack of economic security in their post-war civil employment;
- selection of the Prison Service as a second best after seeking or considering employment in the Police Force, Fire Brigade, or the like.

The strongest common element in these life histories is a concern with stability in family and job relations. This contrasts sharply with the life histories of the sample of thirty-two ordinary prisoners. The feature most common to the prisoners is a history of unwillingness to make sacrifices in order to achieve stability in their family, military service, or job.

The biographies of staff and inmates, speaking generally, present two opposing solutions to the same problems of social adaptation and career choice, in much the same socio-economic setting. Whereas the staff biographies are characterized by predominantly homonomous tendencies,[1] the inmates reveal predominantly autonomous tendencies. A fundamental and persistent characteristic of the prison society is that both staff and inmates appear to be aware of these differences and interpret them as contrasting solutions to common life-problems met in similar socio-economic circumstances. Thus the differences, at least between uniformed staff and inmates, do not normally lead either group to feel that the other is non-human or beyond human comprehension.

---

[1] Homonomy – 'the wish to be in harmony with a unit one regards as extending beyond his individual self' (Angyal, A. *Neurosis and Treatment*, New York, Wiley, 1965, p. 15).

COMMON BACKGROUND, SHARED VALUES, AND MUTUAL EVALUATIONS

These facts of background have relevance in that they point to some of the qualities that officers and inmates bring with them into the prison. The obvious differences that lead some men to volunteer for uniformed service and others to be sent to prison tends to mask other more subtle differences and, in particular, to mask those similarities in outlook that give real significance to the perceived differences. In so far as they come as adult men from the same society, they bring into the prison certain common values and standards that influence their mutual evaluations and hence their behaviour towards each other. It is suggested that the extent of these common values is greater because both officers and inmates typically grew up in working-class families (although not necessarily in the same kinds of neighbourhoods), went to the same kinds of schools, and experienced similar problems of economic insecurity. There are reasons for believing that these values are relevant to an understanding of what happens in a prison, to any change in prison life, and to the selection of staff. The formal definitions of how staff and prisoners shall behave do not, by any means, define the totality of the relations they develop in their day-to-day life. In the informal elaboration and standardizations of their relations, both parties are undoubtedly influenced by their personal qualities. At the same time, shared values, even if they do not carry much weight in any particular instance, do have the character of persistent, impersonal psychological forces. It is this persistence (one might say omnipresence) and apparent objectivity that enable shared values to exert on emerging social relations an influence that is out of proportion to the strength with which they are held.

One of the striking features of the evaluations that staff and men make of each other is the extent to which these are based on common or complementary values. Thus one finds that certain officers and certain types of prisoner are evaluated in the same way by staff and inmates. Moreover, many evaluations that appear to differ can be shown on exploration to derive much of their potency from *commonly held values*. Unless there were such strongly held common values, one suspects that inmates and staff alike would be very much less

D

sensitive to the implicit, and sometimes explicit, criticism they make of each other.

In the mutual evaluations of officers and inmates, the first consideration derives from the fact that the latter have been sent to prison for committing a crime. Social values specifying the immorality of a crime seem to be commonly held by both officers and inmates. Despite the theoretical speculations about 'criminal cultures', which divorce crime of any moral significance, there was little evidence in this case to suggest that the inmates regarded their crimes as anything other than immoral. Thus criminal offences that are socially regarded as being most immoral, e.g. sexual offences against minors, are similarly regarded by officers and prisoners. Inmates committed for these kinds of offences tend to be equally condemned and ostracized by staff and prisoners on moral grounds. Newspaper reports of crimes of this nature evoke similar emotions among staff and inmates. Other offences which carry little moral significance in the outside world, particularly among the working classes (brawling, drunkenness, motoring offences), are found to be equally free from moral condemnation among staff and prisoners. Between these extremes, it still remains true that the bulk of the prisoners, imprisoned for crimes against property, are morally condemned by staff.

Against this personal devaluation the inmates have, as a whole, no direct defences. By their own moral standards they also stand condemned. By strong overt condemnation of the more guilty among them, they make clear they are not guilty of the extremes of immorality but, by the same token, underline their lower level of guilt. Some individuals use the personal defence of claiming to be innocent of the crimes for which they are committed. It is relatively rare for an individual to believe this of himself, and it is a claim that evokes little sympathy among other inmates unless it is extremely well substantiated. The primary defence of the inmates against this devaluation by the uniformed staff is twofold: counter-charge and self-justification. The counter-charge is that the staff themselves must be guilty of some personal moral weakness or else they would not voluntarily have placed themselves in the role of prison warder. This is a very real moral charge, even if conveyed only by implication or innuendo. In our present society there is a widespread belief that the man who is directly responsible for 'caging in' his fellow-men is thereby guilty of immorality. The officers themselves are aware of the widespread existence of this attitude in the community and consequently are keenly sensitive of their own defences against this slight.

The self-justification of the inmates in the face of the moral charge against them is essentially that, while they have done wrong and probably intend to go on doing wrong, this is not simply because they lack these values but because they attach greater importance to other human values. In particular, they would claim to lay great value on individual autonomy, that is, the fulfilment of individual desires in the face of a hostile and unrewarding environment. This defensive self-evaluation generates a further way of devaluing the officers.

'Security' figures large in the officers' reasons for choosing their jobs and in the inmates' perceptions of the officers. The officers are devalued by the inmates on the grounds that they must be the sort of men who would voluntarily sacrifice their autonomy for economic security. By contrast, their self-evaluation in terms of their lawless autonomy is enhanced, and they do not tend to think that their lot in life (as distinct from their lot in prison) is any worse than that of the officers. The officers see the sacrifice of their autonomy (they tend to accept the same cultural valuation of personal autonomy) as a positive and mature contribution to the well-being of their immediate dependents and to that of society at large, in that they have taken on a necessary and difficult social role. However, autonomy retains its high value for the staff and they remain sensitive to inmate devaluation on this score. Their sensitivity will be greater if they feel that their sacrifice is unacknowledged by society or if they do not possess an earlier career that 'proves' their autonomous drives. The latter is not, however, a simple defence. Men who have voluntarily exposed themselves to the extreme situations of wartime commando operations, etc., may feel very anxious to combat their needs for dependency and hence be easily stung by inmate criticisms on this score.

One direct way for an officer to cope with this contradiction is to emphasize the elements of autonomy in his job: to create within his role an area of behaviour that clearly stems from his decisions and to oppose to the security of tenure the insecurity and dangers of the work. These two personal measures tend to go together. Thus from observation of the Bristol staff, it would seem that those officers who share with the inmates a high valuation of personal autonomy are those likely to take up the challenge of the inmate devaluation of themselves on this score by actively exercising their power against the inmates. They will feel most challenged and hence most anxious to pit themselves against the particular inmates who make the most show of their own autonomy. It is not necessary for the inmate to show this by openly breaking the rules. It is enough that he shows by his posture and attitude that he 'thinks he is someone' for him to be marked down by some staff members as a target for their attentions, as someone 'who'll have to have the mickey taken out of him'. It is almost as if there is a slouch and a look of submission that a new inmate has to adopt if he wishes to avoid attention of this kind. A personal variant of this initial testing-out was explained by one such autonomous striving officer: 'You can quickly get an idea of a man's character. You walk straight into the new man's cell and tell him what's wrong, you know – "What's that picture doing on the wall?" "Why is that thing not in its place?"'

Assertion of autonomy through bossing the inmates about is not a generally successful way of coping with anxiety about one's autonomy nor of gaining the respect of other men. It has to be continually reasserted, and any respect thus gained has to be defended against the secondary charges that the show of autonomy is a fake and that it is personal misuse of power that resides in the office, not in the person. This accusation seems to be implicit in the recurrent threats by inmates 'to see him outside'; threats that are sometimes made overtly and sometimes credited by inmates as being effective.

From the staff viewpoint, the career of the ordinary prisoner is not simply that of a working man punctuated by criminal acts and imprisonment; it is a criminal career, a way of life chosen or drifted into, not because the criminals fail to see that crime is normally wrong but despite this, because of a basic distaste for work and a belief that 'work is a mug's game'. This staff belief does not correctly reflect the outlook of all the inmates, but then the staff does not maintain this attitude in every case. There is, however, sufficient reality in it to invoke a cultural criterion of manhood that cannot be entirely rejected by the inmates. Where an inmate has been imprisoned for trying to get something without working for it, there are some grounds *ex post facto* for the suspicion that he could not have obtained it by work even if he had wanted to. The inmates are, for the most part, not strangers to the notion that a man is not a man unless he has some basic skills in coping with and mastering the physical world around him. Their sensitivity to this is revealed in the frequency with which they condemn the prison system for failing to give them real men's work (despite the obvious paradox that they avoid any such thing in the outside world), and by their readiness to condemn the staff for electing to do work which is not really men's work, that is, electing to supervise men rather than work with things, and, in some instances, to direct against an officer the extreme charge of having taken this job because he was a failure in the ordinary work field.

In the preceding discussion, little more has been done than to note some of the complexities involved in the mutual evaluations of staff and inmates. Without further systematic study, it is difficult to assume that the evaluations generally occur in the way outlined. The key proposition does, however, seem fairly certain, namely, that there is a common set of values, particularly about the criteria of manhood, that both staff and inmates bring in from the outside society; that the degree of similarity is enhanced by the fact that the bulk of the uniformed staff and inmates come from the working classes; and that these values play a formative role in the emergence of a psychological environment shared mutually by inmates and staff. In so far as these values emerge from a particular shared cultural and social environment, they are too easily overlooked by those entrusted with the management and development of prisons and, if not overlooked, are still difficult to change. It is a problem faced by any internal security force and historically seems to have been tackled most effectively by:

(a) recruitment of staff from parts of society least likely to share the values of those who are to be controlled, e.g. from rural areas and from men with long-term armed service.

(b) by the segregation of the staff from the community at large, e.g. by barracks, rotation of duties, uniforms, and hours of work.

These problems will not be systematically explored in subsequent pages. They have been highlighted at this point in order to clarify certain characteristics of Bristol Prison that were not changed in this experiment and yet may have exerted an influence on the effects that followed the changes. Thus, if the type of inmate or officer had been different or if they appraised each in terms of different values, it is likely that the changes would have produced different results.

3 · The planned, unplanned, and expected changes

PLANNING THE CHANGES

The broad purpose of the project was to examine the effects of introducing the Norwich system of prison organization into Bristol Prison. A replication in detail was not expected to be feasible, and preliminary studies were undertaken to decide to what extent and in what way the system could be introduced.

The Norwich system involved two changes from the normal pattern of Local Prisons:

(a) A daily routine allowing inmates to spend most of their waking hours outside their cells in association with each other. Incidental to this, a greater amount of time is made available for work, but, as will appear later, there is no evidence to suggest that this makes any significant difference between the Norwich system and the normal pattern.

(b) A change in the officers' responsibilities for inmates. Pairs of officers were made jointly responsible for approximately sixteen named inmates. These responsibilities entailed:

(i) collecting the reception letter from the inmate and, if necessary, helping him to write it;

(ii) making a personal written report on each new prisoner allocated to them, this being done within the first week;

(iii) making such other verbal reports as the governor requests;

(iv) assisting the prisoner with any letters or petitions if such help is required;

(v) writing a final report on each prisoner for the Discharged Prisoners' Aid Society.

In order to design the Bristol scheme, it was necessary to explore the realities of the Norwich system. Preliminary study of that system in operation in Norwich revealed a pattern of changes that appeared to be related to these measures:

(a) There was no overall decline in disciplinary incidents, but the general impression of staff and governor was that these charges were now valid ones and not simply a cover for some long-standing antagonism. There was an unexpected implication that if the total did not decline with the decline in 'cover' charges, then there must have been some increase in genuine incidents. The key implication was, however, that 'long-standing antagonisms' between individual officers and inmates had tended to become a thing of the past, i.e. that an important change had been brought about in the officer-inmate relation. This implication was supported by the next two observations.

(b) A marked decline in the incidence of cell 'smashups'. These incidents can be safely taken as an indicator of tension and, while any individual 'smashup' may be contrived by the inmate, it is only likely to be a successful deceit because most 'smashups' represent a genuine pathological breakdown in personal controls over aggressive hostilefeelings. The frequency of their occurrence in a prison is a crude indicator of tension and hostility of staff–inmate relations.

(c) Observation during association periods showed officers continually and quite freely approached by inmates. These approaches aroused no particular interest in other inmates or officers who happened to be nearby.

(d) Medical complaints had not altered in frequency but less often represented an attempt to escape from prison pressures (e.g. by going 'special sick' during the day to avoid the workshops) and more frequently were 'tryouts' to see how far the new concern for inmates could be taken.

(e) The increase in interaction between inmates was paralleled by the growth of broader inmate groupings – some based on residential locality. These groups were reported to have given some protection from bullies and other exploitative elements. The inmates were, according to the staff, more influenced by the fellow inmates than before, and showed much less tendency to 'do their bird alone'.

These changes seemed to be more closely related to the increased association than to the modification of the officers' responsibilities towards the inmates. The conclusions arrived at after studying the latter measure can best be reported by quoting from the research notes made immediately after the visit to Norwich and before the decisions on Bristol:

These responsibilities [for understanding personal help to inmates] give an officer extra duties of report-writing. This is not generally appreciated by them: the initial reports tend to be vague. Some officers complain that they cannot perform their ordinary duties and also see enough of their charges. There is also an added responsibility for observing, more or less systematically, as the opportunity arises, the men under their charge. *The former responsibilities may lead officers to take a personal interest in their charges but there is little evidence of this except in the few cases willing to accept help with letters and petitions.* Although there was little direct evidence, it may be that the latter responsibilities have resulted in the prisoners being brought under closer scrutiny than would otherwise be the case. With the greater tolerance of inmate interaction, there appears to have been a falling-off in the officers' vigilance or interest. Closer observation of the individual prisoner's character may thus be necessary to forestall abuse of the increased freedom of the system.

Steps were also taken in the workshops to increase the opportunities for staff to have 'helpful conversations' with the inmates. More latitude was allowed for prisoners to converse with each other or to approach the staff. The overseers' stands were abolished and the officers encouraged to move casually around the shop. It was observed, however, that the 'situation is public and oriented to work so that even the best of the trade officers find few occasions on which they can hold a discussion of a prisoner's problems. The main effect seems to be an absence of restraint on the flow of small-talk, normal to the foreman–worker relationship in industry. Compared with the trade officer, the ordinary officer seems to have little basis on which to establish contact with the prisoners in the work situation, and the constraints of this situation offer him little opportunity to observe the men's character.'

These observations on the scheme in operation at Norwich were confirmed in the main by briefer visits to the Oxford and Shrewsbury Local Prisons, which had converted to the Norwich scheme. They suggested that:

(a) There probably were positive effects arising from the Norwich scheme, in particular, a reduction in the general level of tension and an improvement in officer–inmate relations.

(b) The possibility of negative effects could not be ruled out, particularly with respect to inter-inmate relations and vigilance of the staff.

(c) The introduction of the personal counselling component into the officer's role did not appear to contribute to the positive effects but could be suspected of contributing some negative effects.

Regarding the last point, it should be noted that the increased association achieved its positive effects by allowing a greater psychological distance between the officers and inmates (owing to the relatively greater amount of inmate–inmate interaction and less compulsion to personal staff–inmate feuds). On the other hand, the officer counselling was supposed to achieve its effects by decreasing the psychological distance.

Despite the apparent paradox, it is theoretically possible that association might create conditions whereby officers and men might come closer together on a voluntary and more cooperative basis. However, our observations suggested that this view was open to question. It seemed just as likely that the disciplinary duties of an officer were antithetical to such a counselling role. This question could not be settled before study, so it was considered preferable to introduce association and then see whether the change in atmosphere and possibly the disciplinary role permitted experimentation with officer counselling.

Certainly from a practical viewpoint it was undesirable to introduce officer-counselling into Bristol before some change had taken place in the prevailing staff–inmate relations. As is discussed later in this chapter, the dominant staff attitude to further improvements in the prisoner's lot was such that insisting upon additional counselling duties at this early stage would tend to undermine staff willingness to maintain an adequate level of security and internal order within the new system. Whether it might at a later stage be necessary in the interests of security, or desirable for the status of the staff or the reform of the prisoners, to introduce officer counselling could be decided only after seeing whether such duties were reconcilable with other duties of a disciplinary officer in maintaining security and order in a prison with association.

The planned changes at Bristol were thus restricted to a change in the daily timetable so that inmates had their meals and spent a considerable part of the leisure-time in association with each other. Several major restraints affected the organization of the new staff:

(a) too few staff to permit a full two-shift system and barely enough to man the prison for the twelve hours (approximately 7 a.m. to 7 p.m.) in which it was opened up;

(b) regulations laid down for two daily exercise periods, meals, and minimum hours of work;

(c) shortage of even the simplest undifferentiated living-space in which to allow associated eating and leisure activities.

To meet the restrictions of space in the main block of the prison ('A' Hall), it was necessary to limit association to alternate days – two landings on association one day and two the next. Alternating within the one day was rejected as unsatisfactory for inmates who, once they built up social relations, would wish to communicate and associate together at shorter intervals. It was not thought that the proposal for alternate days would lose in any significant way the benefits that seemed to have accrued to the Norwich scheme. Inmates would still have considerable opportunity for being out of their cells and developing and sustaining social relations with other inmates. Their choice of friends would be restricted, but considering the trivial bases of the prison friendships this was not thought to be a serious restriction. The two-day cycle of life for the inmate might lessen boredom and encourage the continuance of private, personal interests in educational classes and hobbies. One more important consideration was taken into account – the absence of separate rooms allowing different leisure activities to be pursued in the condition of quietness and relative privacy most appropriate to them. Where the only available space is restricted and yet undifferentiated in these respects, there is a limited number of persons who can optimally use the space for purposeful activities. Beyond this number, the crowding may restrict such uses, encourage more of the occupants to limit themselves to conversational huddles (as in a crowded public bar), increase the likelihood of fighting, and provide a cloak from official observations. While there were no empirical rules or tables on which to decide this matter, there was common agreement that, even if there were more available space on the ground floor of 'A' Hall, it would defeat the ends of association to have as many as 180 men on association at one time.

Timetabling and staffing difficulties were met in such a way as to produce the changes in the daily activities represented approximately in the following diagram. To avoid undue complexity, the diagrams do not refer to the slopping-out of toilet buckets, etc., which takes place on the landings between 7.00 and 7.30 a.m. each day. Neither does the second diagram refer to the ten-minute periods after breakfast and lunch association in which men return to their cells. In one respect, the week-day contrast is not as sharp as presented in the diagrams: evening classes were also available before the change and enabled the inmate to be out of his cell for an hour or so to engage in education, handicrafts, or musical appreciation.

At the weekend, the contrast is much greater. Before the change, the period from ending work on Saturday mid-day to Monday morning was broken only by a church service, exercise, and a film about once each month (fortnightly at best). In the inmate interviews,

Figure 2 The changes in the daily pattern

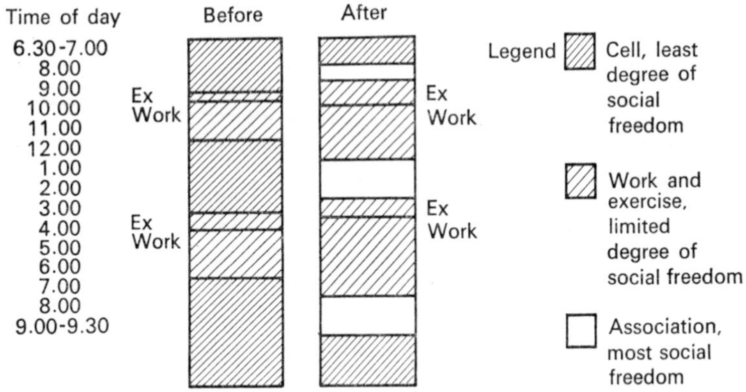

this was commonly referred to as the hardest period of the week to endure. Only a minority were so absorbed in their personal pursuits or so insensitive as to be unworried by the prospect of the next weekend in cells.

After the change there were, in addition to exercise, religious services, and films, the periods of association. 'Evening association' started earlier on Saturdays and Sundays and, although finishing at 6.30 p.m., allowed 3 and $2\frac{1}{2}$ hours respectively for joint activities.

The above discussion of changes has been focused upon 'A' Hall, the main wing of the prison. However, 'A' Hall and 'D' Hall are in certain important respects two different prisons and, at the principal officer level and below, are managed as such. They differ in respect to:

(a) the number and type of inmates
(b) the level of tension
(c) the available space for association.

The same Bell Scale (schedule of daily activities) was introduced for both halls but, because of 'D' Hall's small population and greater relative space, it was possible to allow daily association of its inmates. At any one time, the total on association was less than the number of Ordinaries on association in 'A' Hall.

In addition, it was possible to provide a separate annex for the association of the boys. This space was provided with its own table tennis and a small library. The problem of controlling this annex was rendered easier by the fact that it was open at one end and close to the principal officer's office. More personal control was assured by allocating to it a specially selected officer directly responsible in this matter to the deputy governor.

PREDICTED EFFECTS OF THE CHANGES

The changes described above constitute a substantial increase in the space of free movement for the great majority of the inmates:

1. The narrow confines of the cells cease to be the dominant feature of every day (assuming a 6.30 a.m. to 9.30 p.m. day, 60 per cent of an ordinary week day would be spent in the cells. On association days under the scheme, this would be below 25 per cent).

2. Almost four hours are available every second day in which to mix with other inmates, with complete freedom of conversation and opportunities for engaging in leisure pursuits. These include reading the papers, listening to the radio, playing dominoes, chess, darts, or table tennis.

3. The conditions also enable men to form a wider range of friendships and to sustain them with frequent open contact and joint participation in games.

4. The environment itself changes its appearance for the inmates,

not simply representing an increase of something already offered. Association emerges as a further area inside the prison alongside the cell, the exercise yard, and the work-places. Hence the psychological environment is more varied and less boring. With association, the range of behavioural settings in the prison more closely corresponds to that existing outside and hence should tend to reduce individual suffering.[1]

For the staff there are no such direct satisfactions from the changes. The immediate effects are the extra duty of supervising association and the arrangements for overtime payment, or time in lieu, for evening association.

Upon the basis of social-scientific findings, it was possible to make several predictions about the probable effects of the changes:

1. *The general level of tension would be lower*

   Changes (1) and (4) listed above would both tend to reduce the individual feelings of being hemmed in and unjustifiably deprived. By lowering the level of emotionality, those changes would raise the threshold of the individual to specific frustrations and lessen his tendency to react emotionally to apparent slights. This effect is dependent upon the existing level of tension and the possibilities for achieving additional outlets because of changes. If the existing level of tension were considerably lower and if new goals appeared on the inmate horizon because of the changes, then a higher level of tension might well occur. With the high prior level of tension in Bristol, the changes were regarded as most likely to produce a lowering of the tension. It was not predictable whether the increase in new desires on the part of inmates would offset, in terms of number of offences, the expected decrease in offences in which there is a clash of wills (e.g. a flat refusal of a specific command or abuse of an officer). The lowering of the general level of tension was also expected to be manifested in fewer cell smash-ups and a reduced tendency to go 'special sick' during the day. In addition, one would expect that the change in tension should be experienced as such by inmates and staff.

2. Provided the officers did not adopt a markedly *laissez-faire*

[1] Farber, M. L. 'Suffering and Time Perspective of the Prisoner', *Studies in Topological and Vector Psychology III. Univ. Io. Stud. Child Welf.*, 1944, **20**, 153–227.

attitude, *the inmates would not tend to use the greater freedom provided by association to abuse the regulations or each other.*

One would expect the level of incidents to be lower (and certainly no higher) than before the change, in the relatively less free exercise period, on the assumption that the level of tension (as manifested by the rate of occurrence of disciplinary incidents) is primarily due to the relative deprivation of the inmates. Association would reduce this sense of deprivation and hence lower the level of tension. This is a critical although negative prediction. However, the majority staff view was that the existing tension arose primarily from the personal characteristics of the inmates and that any increase in freedom would be exploited or misused by them, thus necessitating stronger counter-measures and resulting in a still higher level of tension. Many of the inmates saw the level of tension as something resulting from the personal characteristics of the staff and hence believed that any additional period out of the relative security of the cell would only expose the inmates to more persecution and, hence, higher tension. The staff and inmate views were not simply a mirror-image of each other. They had in common the belief that the persistent exploitative minority ('barons' and 'toughs') would seize upon the greater opportunities for exploiting other inmates. If these staff and inmate assumptions were correct, we could expect the periods of association to be marked by more conflict than already occurred in the less free exercise situation.

3. *The officer–inmate relation would become not only less tense but more stable.*

Three things should contribute to this:

(a) The officers will tend to be less central in the life of the inmate. During association, the officer's role is reduced to that of a policeman assuring good order and the inmate does not have to be continually 'looking over his shoulder' as he would on exercise, to see that he is not 'going too slow, too fast, bunching up, whistling, or calling out', or at work, to see that he is not idling, talking too loud in the wrong place at the wrong time, etc. Although association is carried out under the eyes of the officers, there are fewer official requirements to trip up the incautious or indiscreet inmate and less possibility of an officer unjustly charging an inmate. The higher the level of inmate participation in games, the greater the tendency simply to forget about the officers for the time.

(b) The lower the level of general tension, the less likely is an inmate to react emotionally if he is caught out in a particular misdemeanour.

(c) If a certain amount of tension is generated by a particular incident, it is more likely to be dissipated (to lose some of its personal relevance) in participation in association, whereas, before the changeover, it would be something for an individual to brood upon in his cell. Similarly, the development of a wider range of stable friendships would tend to increase the frustration-tolerance of an inmate.[1]

These effects would have an impact upon the staff. They would find that charging an inmate for a simple breach of rules would be less likely to create a tense situation erupting in abuse of themselves and the need to put the inmate on an additional charge under Rule 4. Also the inmate, brooding less over the charge, would not obviously be a case to watch closely and probably charge again in the near future. There would, in other words, be less tendency to a cumulative process in which, if an officer gets caught up in it, personal animosity and fear are generated and bind him and an inmate in a close and personal fashion. It would, on the contrary, be easier for an officer to do his duty and maintain an appropriate distance between his personal feelings and those of an inmate.

4. *Management of officer–inmate relations would become both more feasible and more necessary.*

Management by superiors of the officer–inmate relation is particularly difficult when this relation is inherently unstable and demands personal adjustments by the officer that go beyond his formal role. Thus, if an officer is determined to conscientiously carry out his role, he will have to be prepared to risk the personal animosities of inmates. He may even find it necessary to risk 'half-sheets' (official reprimands) from the governor in order to

---

[1] Wright, E. 'Constructiveness of Play as affected by Group Organization and Frustration', *Character and Pers.*, 1942, **11**, 40–49.

use effective but informal sanctions against certain inmates. The governor must rely on the good sense of his officers to manage the inmates and reserve his powers for the control of informal measures that are too blatant or dangerous. If, on the other hand, an officer refuses to run the risks and personal unpleasantness of a spiral of enforcement and re-enforcement, he can usually evade the pressures from above and may, to placate inmates, unobtrusively flout certain rules. These steps may make an officer's personal situation a little easier, but they automatically reduce the range of the governor's effective authority. If the relation between inmate and officer is rendered less tense and more stable, so that officers can carry out their duties while remaining in role, then it is easier for the governor or his senior staff to manage these roles and hence the behaviour of the officers.

One special management problem does arise if inmate friendships extend in the way predicted. While they create a wider social world for the inmate and make it easier for him to localize difficulties that may arise between him and an officer, they also create certain conditions.[1] The planned changes do not change the essential lack of positive goals about which the inmates might be united and, in fact, the easier life would tend to reduce the sense of sharing a common lot of suffering and common hatred of officers. Hence the bonds within the inmate group will, if possible, be less deep and less binding than before. However, if the inmates are given a common grievance, particularly something out of the ordinary and readily perceivable, then they could far more readily than before communicate their feelings to each other and remonstrate together. Thus, although the individual officer–inmate relations should become less tense and more stable, the inmate group is likely to be, from the viewpoint of the administrator, somewhat less stable and more likely to be disrupted. Such disruption is, however, only likely if there is gross mismanagement in a particular matter (not otherwise, because of the underlying lack of interdependence among inmates); there is no evidence that the intergroup relations would become inherently unstable. Hence it will be more

[1] Polansky, N., Lippitt, R., and Redl, F. 'An Investigation of Behavioural Contagion in Groups', *Hum. Relat.*, 1950, 3, 319–348.

necessary for the governor and his senior officers to control and coordinate the actions of their staff to ensure that mismanagement of this sort does not occur. Food and the handling of feeding arrangements will clearly become critical areas in this respect when done in association.

POSSIBLE UNPLANNED CHANGES

The 'Hawthorne Effect'. Over and above the effects that could be expected to arise from the specific planned changes, it is necessary to consider a general effect that is frequently found to accompany any social change – the so-called 'Hawthorne effect'. Any change instigated by the Prison Commissioners with the apparent intent of improving the lot of the prisoners could be taken by the inmates as evidence of a desire to benefit them or as evidence of the recognition by persons in high places that the inmates have been suffering an injustice that ought to be remedied. In both cases, the changes are interpreted by the inmates as evidence of a positive interest in their lot, but there the similarity ends. If taken as an intended 'benefit', the changes would tend to evoke gratitude; they would be seen as privileges to be earned; and there should be some increased willingness to behave in such a way as to preserve the privileges and induce further benefits from the same source. If taken as a correction of an injustice (e.g. of unjust deprivation of newspapers or freedom of association), there will be no such psychological forces toward gratitude; the effects of the change will be taken as rights, not privileges; and there will be some encouragement to demand recognition of other injustices of their position.

Over recent years, there have been a number of improvements introduced at the instigation of the Prison Commissioners. In the interviews, the attention of the selected sample of ordinary prisoners was specifically directed toward the abolition of the silence rule in the workshops and on exercise, the introduction of the radio and of newspapers, the more liberal provision of library books, the new interior décor (in 1958 the interior was painted in attractive pastel colours), and the Norwich scheme. In each instance, the inmates regarded the change as a partial correction of unfair conditions of imprisonment, not as a gift (only three of the thirty in the sample believed otherwise). Similarly, they viewed the resulting state of

E

affairs as theirs by right and not as a privilege. Consequently, what are officially termed as privileges are not seen as such by the inmates and do not act as positive incentives to good behaviour. What is officially termed punishment by 'loss of privileges' appears to the inmates as straight punishment, not just as a loss of a reward. There was little in what the inmates said in discussion of these changes that could be interpreted as manifesting a sense of gratitude and much that showed that, the more they had, the more they wanted.

The evidence and impressions from this small random sample of Ordinaries was strengthened by the stated views of the staff sample. The recurrent theme in the staff interviews was that these changes and improvements did not evoke gratitude or provide the staff with a set of positive incentives for encouraging the inmates to good behaviour; but they did increase the demand for additional rights.

In an industrial or military organization, the evidence of an interest on the part of the leaders in the lot of the rank and file might well increase the latter's feelings of identification with the organization, even though the specific changes were seen only as deserved justice. However, this possibility hardly exists in the prisons.

From the viewpoint of the inmates, it was unlikely that the introduction of general association would, simply because it was an improvement, lead to a reduction in tension between officers and inmates.

Possibility of a Decline in Staff Morale. A Hawthorne effect is even more unlikely if one also takes into account how the uniformed staff perceive their own interests to be affected. The majority of the staff who were interviewed did not share the strong inmate feeling that the conditions of imprisonment were unjust and they therefore saw the recent improvements (with the exception of the repainting) as benefits bestowed on the prisoners by the Prison Commissioners. Although the majority felt that in some ways the earlier specific changes had made their jobs a little easier, they continued to feel that the inmates were neither particularly deserving nor grateful, i.e. the improvements *per se* tended to harden their negative attitudes to the inmates rather than soften them. The most important effect of the changes was, however, the apparent contrast between the Prison Commissioners graciously bestowing unearned privileges to an ungrateful body of convicted criminals and the same Commissioners giving nothing to their uniformed staff without a struggle. This is a grossly unfair accusation, in that the relations of the two parties to the Commissioners are not comparable. (There is no basis for negotiated settlement of claims between the Commissioners and the inmates, and the time-lag between changes in the general population's living standards and those of the uniformed staff is of quite a different order of magnitude from the time-lag in the case of inmate's living standards.) However, it is a contrast that many of the staff feel compelled to make because of its status implications. To extend privileges to a class of people is to designate them as worthy of higher status. The social status of the disciplinary officers is, in their own eyes, lower than it ought to be, and yet in these changes they see the Commissioners raising the relative status of the inmates. This feeling has been reinforced because in each change they can see a clear intention to help the inmate, but rightly or wrongly, they could see no intention to help the officer or even to save him from extra work or danger arising from the changes.

The scheme for generation association was therefore being introduced under conditions where a Hawthorne effect could not be expected among the inmates and where the staff morale might be deleteriously affected by the change.

MEASURES TAKEN TO INTRODUCE THE CHANGE UNDER REQUIRED CONDITIONS

The mechanics of implementing the planned scheme involved no critical problems. The staff was an experienced body of men, used to working together and with considerable experience of association, both in the limited form available to 'stage prisoners' in Locals and the more general form in Central Prisons. Visits by small staff working parties to Norwich and Shrewsbury provided the basic facts required to draw up a Bell Scale and organize furnishings, games, and feeding arrangements. Many small problems could be expected to arise with the new system – particularly with respect to the increased movement, security, and the cleaning of cells, but provided there was a willingness to operate the scheme efficiently, there was no predictable snag.

The only special measures thought necessary to introduce the inmates to the scheme were a brief orientation by the governor and provision to enable individual inmates to abstain from association.

These measures were adequate because of the absence of shared grounds among the inmates for resistance to the change and because the timetabling of the changes made their communication simple. The most difficult planning problem was the possible deterioration of staff morale. If morale declined for reasons unconnected with the specific nature of the changes being planned, it would not be possible to assess the effects of these changes. The planned increase in space of free movement could be significantly decreased if the uniformed staff felt inclined to take out their grievances against the inmates and, by a general tightening-up, also to bring home to them that, whatever the apparent change in relative statuses, the realities of prison remained unaltered. Space of free movement could also be decreased if a decline in morale led officers to neglect their duties to suppress antisocial behaviour between inmates. Under the latter circumstances, the scheme would mean only increased space of free movement for an exploitative minority.

It was thus unavoidable that, with the prevailing staff attitudes, this study had to be concerned not only with the effects of increased association but also with the conditions required to bring about these changes. Whereas the effects of increased association could be ascertained by comparison with the situation beforehand and by comparison between 'A' Hall and 'D' Hall, no such comparison exists for the appraisal of the attempts to influence staff attitudes. In this latter case, one can only argue from the generality of the determinants that appear to be involved. It is necessary to distinguish between staff attitudes towards change in general and attitudes to the particular change of increased association. For the purposes of assessing the effect of increased association for the inmates, it would have been undesirable to take special steps to change the attitude of the staff toward this measure. However, for reasons discussed above, it was equally necessary to minimize any general distaste for change if the scheme were to be tested under normal conditions of role performance. If the measures to offset staff bias against changes in general went beyond this to induce positive attitudes towards the particular planned changes, then there would be a certain difficulty in interpreting the results of the change in association.

The measures taken to overcome the general bias were:
(a) Setting up a governor's working party from the staff to visit Norwich and examine the scheme in operation there and, sub-

sequently, to bring together staff suggestions about the matter.

(b) An orientation lecture by the governor to all the uniformed staff just before the introduction of the scheme.

(c) The explanation to all of the officers (and inmates) interviewed in connection with the study that the Commissioners intended to judge the scheme on its value for both staff and inmates and not simply for inmates.

These measures yielded no obvious signs of success. Personal contact with the Norwich staff only slightly decreased fears about loss of security and additional work-load, partly because individuals in the visiting party drew different conclusions and partly because of an inclination to discount Norwich experience as due to special circumstances of staff rates and 'tame' inmate population. The 'working party' failed to become fully effective as a joint enterprise; partly because of local tradition of staff relations and partly because of the prison organization. Not surprisingly, the governor, his senior officers, and the P.O.A. branch felt constrained to work in their traditional separate grooves, each looking at the same problem with their own concerns foremost. When they came together, each usually found that the others appeared to be irrational in their expectations and irritatingly unable to see the viewpoint put by him. From limited knowledge of the earlier history of staff relations in Bristol and of the measures taken to introduce the Norwich scheme in two other Local Prisons, it seems that this particular example of staff relations was not unique to the personalities involved. Even in the most successful of the known cases, the change was agreed upon by a process of 'horse-trading' with a minimum of *joint* analysis of requirements. It is probable that the difficulty of establishing a joint working party reflected the general difficulties of governing a prison in which the disciplinary staff is forced out of role, and hence to some degree out of control by the governor, in order to do their jobs. Under these circumstances, the prison as it exists for the disciplinary officers is different from that which exists for the governor in his role – different in ways that encourage misunderstanding. The explanations of the purpose of the scheme given during the interviews did not appear to be any more successful. Although considerable stress was laid upon this, there was insufficient concrete evidence to convince the staff that their needs had been considered or that the scheme would be discontinued if they found it onerous. The one important positive effect achieved by the staff discussions and the orientation lecture was to create a widespread belief that, after a trial period, the scheme would be reappraised and modified as necessary. This gave some protection to the scheme for its initial period but merely postponed the solution of staff problems arising from it.

The available evidence suggests that these measures, although not particularly successful in their aim, at least did not create the added difficulty (for the research; it would be no added difficulty for the administration) of changing attitudes to the content of the scheme. No one on the prison staff was observed to be actively canvassing the scheme, and the research worker tried to avoid giving any impression of bias one way or the other (although it was taken for granted by some of the staff that, as a social scientist and outsider, this was the sort of 'idealistic' thing he would naturally approve). Thus, before the change, two-thirds of the interviewed staff were dubious about or unfavourably disposed towards the scheme. The minority that had some favourable expectations of the scheme presented, with one exception, a consistent pattern that rules out any question of their attitude being due to the interview or any other recent influence. The conditions theoretically required for introducing the change (so that it could be assessed) were not fully achieved. However, they were approximated closely enough for the early stages at least to be assessed. It was unlikely that the success or failure of the scheme would be attributable to unwillingness of the staff to try to operate it or to prior propaganda for the particular scheme.

4 · The changes observed in Bristol Prison

MEASURING THE EFFECTS OF THE CHANGE

Defining the Transition Periods

There was, naturally enough, a period after introduction of the changes during which conflict between staff and inmates ran at a high level. Neither staff nor inmates had been prepared for the new realities and they had to seek a new level of accommodation to each other. Among the inmates, there was a widespread feeling that everything would now be easier; long-standing grievances would be met; the staff was under orders to mother them. At the same time, many inmates felt that their extra hours of work were an unjust imposition and that the staff would rob them of the new liberties by declaring the scheme unworkable. The staff shared common feelings about the apparent disorderliness of the scheme, the tightness of the early time schedule, and the fact that for them the most marked of the early effects of the scheme was an increased load of evening duties that had to be 'paid-off-in-time' during the middle of the following day. (On my calculation, the evening duties rose from approximately 0·75 hours to 2·25 per week and to 2·8 per week during the summer, owing to officers taking leave.) Staff–inmate relations appeared to have reached a new level of stability within eight weeks.

To be on the safe side (i.e. to avoid undue confusion of transitional effects with long-run effects), a period of eight weeks was allowed for the transitional period and the major comparisons were made between the sixty-four weeks prior to introduction of the change and the sixty-four weeks after the transitional period. Sixty-four weeks was eventually selected because there was a suspicion that seasonal effects operated at least before the change and more importantly, because the new system showed signs of a recurrent five-to-six-monthly 'crisis'. Analysis of the first 'crisis' revealed no special extraneous cause, suggesting a new source of inherent instability with the possibility that, after such a crisis, the system might not return to its previous level. For the earliest part of the period covered, it was possible to get corroborative staff and inmate observations for only a proportion of the disciplinary incidents.

Reported Disciplinary Incidents as a Measure of Staff–Inmate Tension

The officers, in their primary task of enforcing the rules and regulations of the prison, constitute the greatest single set of restraints on the inmates; certainly they are more prominent in the eyes of the inmates than walls and bars or moral restraints. While moral restraints undoubtedly have important persistent effects, they are relatively constant and for that reason easier to come to terms with or to get around by rationalizations of some sort. The restraints exercised by the officers are more persuasive, flexible, and not so readily avoided. Being human, the officers are able to meet stratagem with counter-stratagem; attempts at concealment with searches and informers; subtle belittlement with harassing tactics or informal punishment; violence with violence. Also because they are human, their frustration of inmate strivings is far more likely to arouse interpersonal tensions than would frustration by impersonal forces;[1] and in turn, they are more likely to become a target for inmate hatred, revengefulness, seduction, or trickery. We can expect those frustrating incidents to be particularly salient in the minds of the inmates because they are seen not as accidental but as part and parcel of prison life.[2] As has been repeatedly found in studies of schools,[3] it does not greatly matter if one is not personally involved in these incidents: their occurrence is a reminder of the threatening nature of the prison world.

Disciplinary incidents thus refer to the core of the relation between officers and inmates. (This would cease to be so only if the primary task of the officers *vis-à-vis* their charges were different, e.g. educa-

---

[1] See Heider, F. 'Social Perception and Phenomenal Causation', *Psychol. Rev.*, 1944, **51**, 358–374. 'Usually frustration leads to aggression only (and not always even then) when the origin of frustration is attributed not to one's own person or to impersonal causes, but to another person' (p. 370).

[2] Heider, *ibid.*, p. 371, ' . . . frustration is experienced as a threat to the personality only when it is interpreted in terms of the social environment; that is to say, when persons are perceived as the origins of the frustration and the temporary deprivation is related to durable environmental relevancies.'

[3] Oeser, O. A., and Emery, F. E. *Social Structure and Personality in a Rural Community*, London, Routledge & Kegan Paul, 1954.

tional, therapeutic, production supervising, or merely movement-control.) A reported disciplinary incident represents a particular instance of power exercised by an officer over an inmate with, in most cases, some resulting punishment for the inmate.

It is a general principle of social science that the level of tension between two social groups will be manifested by the frequency and intensity of their conflict.[1] There is the exceptional case in which a social situation is so highly repressive that the frequency of *overt* conflicts (disciplinary events) no longer reflects the level of tension and other indices have to be sought.[2] However, this level of repression (while not uncommon in families and classrooms) is infrequently found in penal establishments and even concentration camps. In a Local Prison, such highly repressive atmospheres only occur for very fleeting instances, e.g. when a public display of force has been necessary to restrain an inmate gone berserk. One such instance occurred in Bristol some twelve months before the change and was followed by a flood of petitions by the inmates but a marked temporary drop in disciplinary incidents.

The frequency of disciplinary offences in all Local Prisons is evidence that:

(a) their regimes are not exceptionally repressive, and

(b) staff–inmate conflict is normal.

Hence, apart from rare occurrences, it is reasonable to expect that the frequency and intensity of overt conflicts will reflect the level of tension in staff–inmate relations.

Beyond these general principles is a number of specific problems involved in the use of disciplinary incidents as an index of tension. Two variations in staff–inmate behaviour can be discounted as significant distortions of the index: first, the question of the guilt of the inmate; second, the case where a breach of rules is committed but not observed or, if observed, not reported. In the former case, the reported incident constitutes a conflict between the officer and the inmate and manifests some social tensions leading them into conflict,[3]

---

[1] See the discussion of quasi-stationary equilibrium in Chapter IX of Lewin, K. *Field Theory in Social Science,* N.Y., Harper, 1951; London, Tavistock.

[2] Lewin, K., *ibid.*

[3] The question of whether or not the inmate is guilty concerns the tension generated by the conflict rather than the tensions manifested by and preceding the conflict.

while in the latter the incident is not in the same sense a conflict. If this were the norm in a given prison, one would expect to find a low level of staff–inmate tension paralleling the low level of reported incidents. (It would not, of course, be a model prison.)

There are, however, two serious problems in the use of disciplinary incidents as an index of tension. The first is the existence of informal forms of conflict. 'Going slow', sarcasm, ridicule, 'needling', etc., are constantly being used between staff and inmates. Although an experienced staff can deal out a number of informal punishments, they are effectively restrained by their own discipline and by fear of dismissal from any frequent use of severe informal punishments. Consequently, the staff will go to some trouble to bring any informal conflict into the official channels (i.e. 'to put a man on report') where the offending inmate can be officially punished. Thus, unless the basic-grade disciplinary staff is 'out of control', it is most unlikely that informal conflicts will replace formal conflicts to an extent rendering the latter invalid as an index. The more important problem, if one goes beyond the first crude approximation of frequency of incidents, is to take some account of the differences in intensity of conflict represented by disciplinary incidents. Each disciplinary charge is classified for internal judicial purposes according to the rule or rules broken. Sufficient additional data were available on the charge sheets or obtainable from inmates and staff to enable all incidents in the 136 weeks under study to be reclassified for our purposes (see Appendix 3). Briefly, it was held on theoretical grounds that the greatest intensity of tension is manifested in direct attacks (usually verbal) against an officer, the next greatest in refusing to obey an order or perform a duty, and the least in incidents where an inmate has been caught trying to further his own ends (e.g. smuggling, writing letters, gambling, stealing). This classification is still crude but it is an improvement on a simple index of frequency of incidents and, for present purposes, probably adequate.

THE OBSERVED EFFECTS IN 'A' HALL

The main effects apparently due to the change will first be presented for 'A' Hall. Because of the differences between 'A' and 'D' halls, the results are presented separately and are regarded as being, in large measure, two separate tests of the planned changes and as defining part of the range of effects that may be expected with different amounts of association and different populations.

As a first step, however, it is necessary to show that association took on for the inmates the social and psychological characteristics that the planners intended it to have. Predictions were based on the assumptions that the periods of association would become periods in which men would willingly engage in joint leisure pursuits and that this would be generally felt to be an improvement in living-conditions. Quite different predictions would be in order if the planners had succeeded only in creating periods of the day, formally labelled 'association', in which the inmates were driven to boredom and unable or unwilling to relax together. This is not a fanciful hypothesis. Some nine of the twenty officers in the sample thought that association might not work because so many of the inmates would prefer to stay in cells. This observation is commonly made in Local and Central Prisons and is supported here by the fact that eighteen of the thirty in the inmate sample expressed doubts about whether they personally wanted association. As put by one inmate, 'The only ones who will want to come out on association are the ones who can't do their bird.' The planning assumption was that this behaviour was an adaptation to the prevailing conditions and would be readily discarded by all but the old inmates who had become institutionalized. Thus, as in any experiment, it is neccessary to establish the real experimental changes to which the effects are to be related.[1]

An indication of what association meant to the inmates is provided by the use they voluntarily made of the games material. A running record was kept by the inmates in charge of issuing the material, and repeated observations enabled us to determine the modal size of the groups engaged in uses of different types of material (where this was not pre-established by rules or cultural usage). It was exceptional for material to be taken out and not be used but common for it to be used by additional groups without being returned and reissued. A measure of re-use could not be obtained, so the resultant index of use (sum of games issued by modal number using each type) is, despite

[1] A question might be raised at this point as to what should be considered experimental changes and what effects. The position taken here is that the entertainment of inmates is no primary task in a prison. The creation of a lively and attractive association has to be judged in terms of its effects relevant to the real primary task of a prison.

the fact that some of the re-users were accounted for by the first games, an underestimate. The degree of underestimation does not appear to vary between the two shifts of inmates going on association, but is greater in the evening period than at lunchtime.

Table 7 – A minimum estimate of percentage of inmates using association materials

	Inmates from 1st and 3rd landings		Inmates from 2nd and 4th landings	
Average for	noon	evening	noon	evening
1st sample	55	55	60	62
2nd sample	56	56	68	71
3rd sample	62	59	71	68
4th sample	56	62	80	86

(These are 3 weekly samples from each of the four sixteen-week sub-periods after the transition period.)

These figures support the compelling impression of frequent personal observations, namely, that the association was, as planned, a period of joint relaxation. The majority of inmates engaged in some game with their fellows, usually in groups of more than two. Over the period, the percentage participating showed signs of slight but steady increase. The consistent difference between the two shifts appeared to be due to no more than the fact that the aged and sick tend to be housed on the first landing (this being the ground floor).

Apart from games of darts, chess, dominoes, and table tennis, inmates could read the papers, talk, watch others play, or listen to the radio. These occupations might betoken idleness. Certainly if most of the inmates were so engaged there would be an unmistakable impression of idleness, and optimum conditions for the growth of cliques and for conversations in which criminal experience and prowess would be central. As shown in *Table 7*, this was not the case. From observation it also seems that there was no substantial minority that consistently refrained from active participation. Only a few individuals came on to association and kept to themselves, and an occasional group of newcomers took a while to settle in to the normal pattern.

The first assumption about association thus appears to have been met in reality.

The second assumption, noted above, was that under the prevailing conditions association would be seen by the inmates to be an amelioration of living-conditions. If, in fact, the inmates wished to remain in their cells and felt association to be an imposition, predictions other than those made in the preceding chapter would be in order. Similarly, if association were so badly organized as to be boring or dangerous, men might feel that the innovation of association made no difference and react accordingly. Both of these hypotheses can be rejected. The inmates had the right to opt out of association and the reality of this choice was demonstrated at the very beginning when a sizeable number exercised this option. This number subsequently declined and at no time were less than seventy per cent of the inmates voluntarily on association.

Table 8 – Percentage of inmates voluntarily on association in 'A' Hall

15 September 1958	73
14 December 1958	76
24 March 1959	80
15 March 1960	75

Each of these figures is an underestimation. Many of those not on association are on duties in the kitchen, hospital, and in the officers' mess and find it inconvenient to go on association. If those are accounted for, only 15 per cent might be regarded as voluntarily opting out of association. Age appears to be the most important single factor: the older an inmate, the less likely he is to volunteer for association ($\chi^2 = 9.2$, df $= 1, p < 0.01$ for all inmates; $\chi^2 = 14.5$, df $= 1, p < 0.01$ for the total, less kitchen and mess staff). Length of sentence appears to be unrelated ($\chi^2 = 1.9$, df $= 1$, n.s. for total, less kitchen and mess staff).

Interviews with inmates who were staying off association showed that they regarded this as a personal quirk or due to personal difficulties with other prisoners. The first point was bluntly put by one old inmate, 'Some queer ones and real old jailbirds do their time behind locked doors because they don't know any other way. They have had too much of the old system.'

The changes in the attitudes of the small inmate sample provide direct evidence that the plans to create an attractive association were, in fact, achieved.

Table 9 – Individual inmate attitudes to association

| | | After the change (December 1958) | | | |
		Favourable	Doubtful	Against	Totals before
Before the change (July 1958)	Favourable	11	—	1	12
	Doubtful	5	1	—	6
	Against	7	2	3	12
	Totals after	23	3	4	30

Of the fifteen who changed their attitudes, all but one became more favourable. Subsequent interviews through 1959 and early 1960 revealed no signs of a swing back. (It is extremely unlikely that these attitudes were due to some unrelated factor. Thus, for instance, earnings and winnings are another source of satisfaction, but only half of the group improved their financial standings in this period – for a modal gain of fivepence.)

When those inmates were asked to consider how association was regarded by the inmates at large (rather than simply how it suited their own circumstances) there was even less ambiguity.

Table 10 – Perceived attractiveness of association for inmates at large – as seen by inmates

| | After | | | |
	Favourable	Doubtful	Unfavourable	Totals before
Before				
Favourable	13	1	—	14
Doubtful	11	1	—	12
Unfavourable	3	—	1	4
Totals after	27	2	1	30

On this matter, the small sample of uniformed staff was almost as unanimous, although initially much less optimistic.

Table 11 – Perceived attractiveness of association for inmates – as seen by officers

	Favourable	*After* *Doubtful*	*Unfavourable*	*Totals before*
Before				
Favourable	9	—	—	9
Doubtful	5	2	—	7
Unfavourable	4	—	—	4
Totals after	18	2	—	20

The staff attitudes showed more variability after December 1958, but the majority remained of the belief that association was of value to the inmates.

The above evidence makes it safe to assume that the planned change was essentially achieved. It remains to examine the observed effects on tension, etc., and to consider whether these can be attributed to the change.

Figure 3   Half-hourly distribution of incidents and opportunities for inmate interaction before change

(Averaged for all weekdays in the 'before' period*)

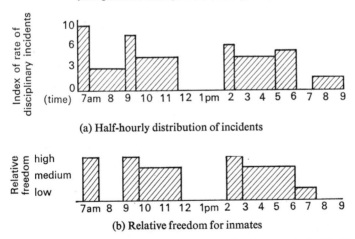

(a) Half-hourly distribution of incidents

(b) Relative freedom for inmates

* The pattern did not differ significantly between the first and the last half of the 'before' period, or among the days of the week for the entire period.

Prediction 1: The effect of increased opportunities for offending

'That in those parts of the day given over to association, the level of incidents would not increase above that previously pertaining in exercise periods.'

It will be recalled that there was an assumption entertained by some of the staff that the rate of occurrence of incidents was simply a function of inmate propensities and opportunities. On this assumption, association looked like an additional opportunity for trouble-making, at least as good as that already provided by associated exercise. Comparison of graphs (a) and (b) below shows that before the change the level of incidents did closely map the occurrence of opportunities – the more freedom for inmate interaction, the higher the rate of incidents – and hence, on the face of it, there were good grounds for this assumption.

After the transition period the rate of occurrence of disciplinary incidents ceased to correspond to the degree of freedom for the inmates [graphs (b) and (c) compared with (d)]. Association was marked by a low level of incidents, exercise ceased to be a focal point, and, apart from the early-morning slopping out, most incidents occurred during work.

As the graphs show, there is no support for the 'opportunities' hypothesis.

The graphs give some grounds for maintaining the interpretation made so far in this study, i.e. that the rate of reported incidents primarily reflects the level of staff–inmate tension. Supporting the evidence presented in the graphs is the absence of pilfering and vandalism of association materials. Up to January 1960, there were no signs of deliberate destruction or damage to tables, chairs, etc., and the games material was still completely intact. The only wear that was noticeable was no more than could be expected with continual, normal use. Similarly, there were no noticed cases of premeditated violence between prisoners. The odd thumps were exchanged in temper (practically confined to the younger men on table tennis) but premeditated violence for debts, etc., was carried out elsewhere.

Against this background of a generally settled association, attention must be directed to a type of incident that had become more likely. Two 'touchy' group situations arose over food during the

Figure 4   Half-hourly distribution of disciplinary incidents and opportunities for inmate interaction after the changeover

(Averaged for all weekdays in each period*)

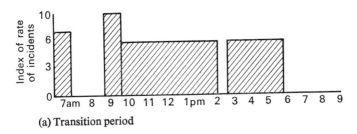

(a) Transition period

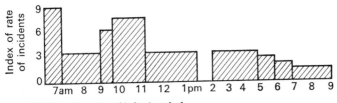

(b) First 14 weeks of 'after' period

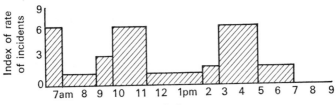

(c) Last 50 weeks of 'after' period

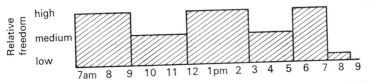

(d) Relative freedom for inmates throughout transition and 'after' period.

(* Only the 50-week period was long enough to permit a statistical test of the stability of the pattern. No significant difference was found between the 1st and 2nd halves of this period, nor between weekdays for the entire period.)

transition situation. I was present during one and was able to reconstruct the first from staff and inmate evidence. In one instance, an item on the menu was distasteful to the inmates and the loud protests of one were quickly taken up, but less loudly, by others. In the other, there was a delay in serving part of the breakfast and, with the little time initially available for breakfast, many of the inmates thought they might miss out. The muttering was growing in intensity until the prompt action of a senior officer overcame the delay. These incidents illustrated what was expected; namely, that if issues of this sort occurred during association, they would spread rapidly and create a group incident. While such group incidents are undesirable because of their subsequent effect on staff–inmate relations, it is most unlikely that they would here produce any rioting. The generally low level of tension was reflected in the relative good temper of the inmate participants in the two incidents and the readiness with which they settled down. There was no feeling among staff and inmates that the particular cause of the incidents was 'the last straw' in a generally bad situation.

One might suggest that group incidents under the conditions prevailing before the change would have been more difficult for the staff to manage.

Even in the transition period it is unlikely that the 'opportunities hypothesis' is valid. As already discussed, the added disturbances of this period seem to be due to temporary confusion of roles, buoyancy of inmates, and temporary lack of standard operating procedures. Organizational difficulties with the breakfast period created pressure on both staff and inmates and continued into the first period after transition, graph (b). The latter phase, graph (c), reflects a lessening of tension with the improved organization of the breakfast period. Unexpectedly, the evening association shows no decline in tension in the later phase. Examination of the incidents occurring at this time shows one new source of conflict, but this is not attributable to the opportunities hypothesis. The evening classes overlap with the last half hour of association and this puts many of the inmates into what may well be an unnecessary conflict situation. In evading classes, they come into conflict with the rules; in attending classes, they break up an ongoing darts or table tennis competition. On these data, it seems that the 'opportunities hypothesis' may safely be put aside.

Prediction 2: The general level of tension

'That the general level of tension will decline.'

A series of answers can be given to this question, each more precise and serving to narrow the meaning of 'general level of tension'.

(a) In terms of total number of reported disciplinary incidents, there is a statistically significant decline after the transition. For the sixteen consecutive four-weekly periods before the change, the mean number of incidents was 16·8 but only 14·0 for the sixteen four-weekly periods after the transition ($z = 2·98, p < 0·01$).

This comparison makes no allowance for changes in the size of the inmate population of 'A' Hall. By common sense, one would expect that more offences would occur with more inmates, particularly when an increase in inmate numbers is not paralleled by a similar increase in staff and facilities to cope with it. Before the change there was indeed a positive correlation between population size and number of incidents ($\tau = 0·42, 0·10 > p > 0·05$), and after the change the population was significantly larger (for median test of the population graph $\chi^2 = 9·30, p < ·01$). Therefore, the effect of population size would seem relevant to the comparison of the before and after periods.

Computing the rate of offences/1000 man-days on the basis of the daily population figures, this rate is found to decline from 2·38 before to 1·66 after. As expected, this sharpens the comparison. With population size taken into account, the ratio of incidents after to incidents before declines from 83 to 70 per cent. Put another way, *if incidents had occurred at the same rate as before, one would have expected 323 incidents – 44 per cent more than actually occurred.*[1]

(b) This gross difference remains a doubtful test of the prediction for several reasons. One is that the total figures refer to both

---

[1] For a similar use of disciplinary data to indicate changes in prison regime see Gunderson, E. K., *et al.* 'Program Effectiveness in Naval Retraining', *Seventh Technical Report*, Rehabilitation Research Project, U.S. Naval Retraining Command, Camp Elliott, San Diego, California, 3 February 1958.

the domestic sector and the work sector of prison life, but the planned changes were confined to the former (apart from a slight increase in hours of work). It is possible that the observed differences in the totals would have arisen from unplanned changes in the work situation (i.e. unplanned from the viewpoint of the experiment, not necessarily from the administrative viewpoint), and not at all from the planned changes. It is even possible that a decrease in incidents at work had hidden an increase in the domestic sector. *Table 12* indicates that these possibilities are not realized. An increase in number of incidents at work has actually operated to mask the full effects of the planned change. Thus, for the domestic sector, without even allowing for the population increase, the incidents after change were only 62 per cent of those before.

Table 12 – Mean rate of disciplinary incidents/4-week period

	Before (*16 periods*)	*Transition* (*2 periods*)	*After* (*16 periods*)	*Significance of the difference between before and after*
Domestic sector	11·6	17·5	7·2	$z = 2·90\ p < ·01$
Work sector	5·25	11·5	6·8	$z = 0·73$ n.s.

It should also be noted that the lack of improvement in the work situation is not necessarily evidence against the proposition of a decline in staff–inmate tension.

While a decline in tension in the domestic sector would be expected to carry over into the work situation, it is also to be expected that the work situation would appear increasingly anachronistic to the inmates and more than ordinarily restrictive. This latter view was strongly expressed not only by the interviewed inmates but also by many of the staff. Some of the early increase in dislike for the work situation can be attributed to the increase in hours worked[1] (without a corresponding

[1] The hours of work increased from 24·35 to 34·45 (this latter is a formality and includes movement time. The author's observations and calculations suggest that it is nearer 32 hours).

increase in earnings), but the persisting dislike seems to be due to the contrast that had developed between it and the domestic situation.

The change in attitude to work is particularly reflected in the increase in fights between inmates while at work (from 10 instances before to 25 after). Investigation of each of these incidents revealed that the increase was accounted for by unpremeditated outbursts, minor provocation, sheer irritability, and bad temper. Unlike so many of the fights before change, these were followed in many cases by genuine regret. Both staff and inmates suggested that there were basic improvements in the atmosphere in the shops owing to the lessening of staff–inmate tension. These views are supported by the fact that the distribution of incidents ceased to show clustering effects and approximated to a random Poisson distribution. (No change was made in the duty rostering of officers for supervisory duties, and hence the change in distribution of incidents was not attributable to staff changes.) After the change, there appeared to be no systematic bias of officers or inmates towards causing trouble or of one incident to trigger off or create the atmosphere for further conflict.

(c) The comparison of totals could also be misleading because of the different types of incidents included. The level of tension is more accurately indicated by those incidents in which the conflict is personal (e.g. abuse or threats directed at the officer) than by those incidents in which an inmate is simply breaking the rules to further his own ends. The total figures include both kinds of incidents, and hence it is possible that tension could decrease quite markedly, as measured by 'personalized incidents' and yet the total number increase because of a big increase in less tense incidents. It is also possible that there could be an increase in 'personalized incidents' and yet the total number decrease because of a decrease in the other incidents (a pattern of change that would most probably mark a real increase in repression). Or there could be no change in the rate of 'personalized incidents' but a decline in the total because of a decrease in other types (which would suggest a decrease in tension due to officers withdrawing from their roles and 'not wanting to know').

In this instance all types of incidents in the domestic sector decreased, but the most marked decline was, significantly, in 'personalized incidents'.

Table 13 – Changes in rate of occurrence of incidents involving verbal or other attacks on officers

| | Mean rate | | Significance of difference | As percentage of all incidents | |
	Before	After		Before	After
Domestic sector	3·50	1·00	$z = 4·2$ $p < ·001$	30·5	13·8
Work sector	1·81	1·94	n.s.	34·6	31·8

Together with the relatively small decline in other types of offences (23 as against 71 per cent), the evidence strongly suggests that there has been no significant withdrawal of officers from their duties. If an officer were inclined to withdraw, he would tend to overlook or ignore simple breaches of rules, but he would not so readily overlook personal attacks.

These data also confirm the preceding evidence of a significant decline in officer–inmate tension in the domestic sector of prison life and lack of change in the work sector.

(d) The changes were not expected to affect all inmates alike. According to the 'social tension' hypothesis the youngest ordinary inmates should feel more sharply than the older ones the deprivations of the regime and be more sensitive to degradations of status. By the same token, they should gain the most relief from association and the decreased salience of their relations with the officers.

This prediction is supported by the data in *Table 14*. Before the change, the youngest of 'A' Hall's inmates contributed two-and-a-half times their share of incidents and the oldest only one-quarter. After the change, the young inmates are relatively less often the source of conflict and the old inmates seem to be less withdrawn.

The differences in the age distributions are statistically significant (χ^2 between before and after $= 12·3$, $p < ·01$). Age and what it implies are still important determinants of the level of tension. Thus, after the change, the age distribution still differs significantly from what would be expected if age

Table 14 – Incidents of offences by age (per cent)

Age	Expected	Observed Before	Observed After	Change
20–24	16	41	28	−13
25–29	25	22	32	+10
30–39	31	30	28	− 2
40+	28	7	12	+ 5
	100	100	100	

were unconnected with the occurrence of incidents ($\chi^2 = 20{\cdot}4$, $p < {\cdot}001$). This age effect is, however, less than existed before the change (when $\chi^2 = 54{\cdot}63$).

(e) A peripheral indicator of the change in tension is provided by the tendency to go 'special sick'. Apart from the daily sick parade for which an inmate enters his name the previous evening, he may also report 'special sick' at any time. It is commonly recognized in the prison that one factor leading to a 'special sick' complaint is a desire to get away from work or some other situation. The observation is frequently made that if tension runs high in a workshop, there will be a rush of 'special sick' complaints. Needless to say, many such complaints are genuine and they cannot readily be distinguished from those that are not.

It seems reasonable, however, to assume that in the prison the rate of 'special sick' complaints will tend to change with the level of tension. At the same time, the rate will change with the total rate of sickness – the more inmates putting down for regular sick parade, the greater the likelihood of some being ill enough during the day to go 'special sick'. For this reason, the most suitable index was thought to be the ratio of 'special sick' to the number on sick parade for the same day. (Attempts were made to distinguish the genuine and spurious 'special sick' but the results were hopelessly inconsistent with other evidence.) This index was computed for three periods – the eight weeks before the change, twenty-two weeks after, and the last nine weeks of the period under study.

Table 15 – Ratio of 'special sick' to total sick

	Before	*After I*	*After II*
Number of weeks above median	7	10	3
Number of weeks below median	1	12	6

This result can be taken only as suggestive. Difficulties that I experienced with classification of the medical data made it unwise to pursue this matter beyond this point.

To summarize the evidence on this proposition, there is a high degree of unanimity among staff and inmates that the general level of tension declined after the change. These beliefs reflect a significant decline in the rate of disciplinary offences in the domestic sector of prison life but not in the work sector. The decline is greatest in those offences that involve aggression, verbal or otherwise, to officers and for those inmates who are under twenty-five years of age. The evidence of a decline in numbers going 'special sick' is at best only suggestive. (Similarly, although smashups were almost nonexistent after the change, they were so infrequent and irregular before, that the period studied was too short to permit statistical testing.)

Prediction 3: Stability of the officer–inmate relation

'That the officer–inmate relation would become less inherently unstable.'

The incidents of personalized conflict nearly all arise after an officer has apprehended or cautioned an inmate for some simple breach of the rules. Hence the data presented above are also evidence of the instability of officer–inmate relations. These data can be expressed as the proportion of total incidents in which routine disciplinary action leads to interpersonal conflict.

In the domestic sector, the chances have shifted from one-in-three to one-in-seven. They remain unchanged in the work sector.

In the earlier theoretical sections, the hypothesis was advanced that this tendency for the routine performance of disciplinary duties to erupt into personal conflict and hostility would create a schismatic tendency in the staff – some officers withdrawing from the danger, and hence from fulfilment of their roles, and others becoming deeply enmeshed in a personal struggle with the inmates, and by the same token less responsible to official controls. If the interpretation placed

Table 16 – Percentage of all incidents that lead to verbal or other attacks on officers

	Before	After
Domestic sector	30·5	13·8
Work sector	34·6	31·8

on the above data is correct, then one should expect to find less of a schism between the 'active' officers and the 'passengers'.

Given the length of time under consideration, the administrative efforts to ensure a fair distribution of duties (jealously guarded by the basic-grade staff), and the relative infrequency of reports per officer/shift, it is reasonable to assume that, if the main determinant of entering a report were simply the chance event of being present when a misdemeanour occurred, the distribution of reports by officers would approximate to a Poisson distribution. As expected, a statistically significant difference existed between the actual distribution for the before period and the Poisson distribution for the same mean (χ^2, for goodness of fit, $= 12\cdot74$, $p < \cdot01$). For the after period, the actual distribution did not differ significantly from the poisson ($\chi^2 = 2\cdot69, 0\cdot90 > p > 0\cdot50$).

Before the change, the number of officers making few or no reports was greater than would be expected if there were no bias on their parts, and the number making many reports was similarly greater. That is, the evidence suggests that there was a schism of the staff into 'actives' and 'passengers' and that the middle position was apparently difficult to maintain. After the change, there is no evidence of such a schism and no absence of officers occupying the middle position. This does not deny that some individual officers continue to be biased in one way or another, but it appears from the evidence quoted that this is exceptional. The general evidence on this point can be supplemented to some extent without getting down to identifiable cases. Thus the following table shows the change for a key clique of 'activists'.

Table 17 – Ratio of actual to expected number of reports for the four top-scoring officers

	Before		After		
Sub-periods	1	2	1	2	3
	3·0	3·3	2·4	1·8	1·7

A similar pattern was seen in the case of 'personalized incidents'. Before the change, these four officers were involved in almost six times as many such incidents as would be expected on chance, afterwards only in twice as many. Before the change, this group was also more deeply involved with reporting the top five inmate offenders than would be expected on chance. After the change, their involvement is no higher than chance. Although a small core of very frequent and serious offenders remains unaffected by the change, this group of officers has apparently managed to disentangle itself from them and also feels less impelled to overfulfil its role.

At several levels, the evidence thus supports the prediction of less instability within the officer–inmate relation. The matter can now be raised at a higher level of generality. If the change in officer–inmate relation is as suggested, then there should be:

(a) less cumulative build-up of tension;
(b) less fluctuation in the level of tension;
(c) a greater stability in the face of external changes; and
(d) smaller differences in staff and inmate attitudes.

(a) *Less cumulative build-up of tension.* Tension may tend to accumulate because the individual incident heightens hostility between the inmate and officer immediately concerned or because it poisons the social atmosphere within which other inmates and staff confront each other. With either or both processes operating, incidents would tend to cluster – the occurrence of one incident would increase the likelihood of another occurring. If these processes are not operating, then incidents could be expected to be randomly distributed between the weeks (not within weeks, since the days differ in the strain placed on staff and inmates). *Table 18* shows that for both the domestic and the work sectors, there has been a shift from a non-random clustering to a random pattern.

Table 18 – Approximation to Poisson distribution of incidents/week

	Before (64 weeks)	After (64 weeks)
Domestic sector	$\chi^2 = 14\cdot25, p < \cdot02$	$\chi^2 = 2\cdot62$ n.s.
Work sector	$\chi^2 = 6\cdot49, p < \cdot05$	$\chi^2 = 1\cdot29$ n.s.

Further evidence suggesting a decline in the tendency for tension to accumulate is provided by the daily distribution of offences within the week. This has not altered for offences at work but, in the domestic sector, a clear difference can be observed. Before the change, the cyclical movement suggests a high initial level of tension falling off on Tuesday, then building up to fall off on Saturday. After the change there is the same high initial level, but then (within the domestic sector) tension falls off throughout the rest of the week. The distri-

Figure 5   The weekly pattern of offences – domestic sector*

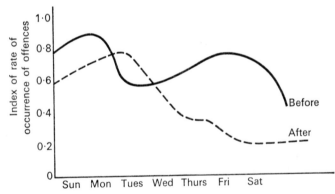

* For both periods, a statistical comparison of the first and last half showed no significant difference.

bution of incidents involving abuse of staff follows the same cyclical pattern before the change, but after the change these incidents are evenly distributed throughout the week.

(b) *Less fluctuation in the level of tension.* The general stability can be hinted at only by a study of the observed fluctuations in level of tension. A graph of the level seems to show a continuous up and down movement before the change and, after the transition, a tendency to run evenly for a period with smooth changes in level and, every six months, a brief upsurge in number of offences. Evidence of less fluctuation should appear in the short-term weekly fluctuations within the four-week periods. The mean range of variation within the 16 four-week periods before is found to be significantly greater than the mean range of variation after (mean range before = 3·75, after = 2·70; z = 3·76, p < 0·01). Analysis of variance shows that the short-term fluctuations account for most of the variance before the change but not after.

The six-monthly upsurge, which has occurred three times since the change (points marked a, b, and c on the accompanying graph), requires special attention. On-the-spot study of what was happening in the prison when the first upsurge occurred led to the hunch that this was no accidental agglomeration of events but a system characteristic that would result in further upsurges about four to six months later. Even though this prediction held true, one could not at the time exclude the possibility that one such upsurge might get out of control

Figure 6

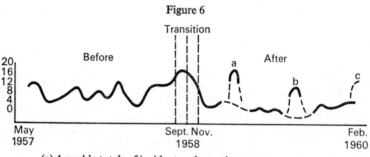

(a) 4-weekly totals of incidents – domestic sector

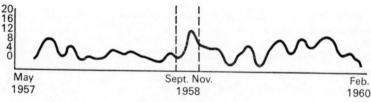

(b) 4-weekly totals of incidents – work sector

and force a reversion to the earlier system. While the evidence for the following interpretation is scanty, some speculation is warranted because of the administrative importance of these fluctuations, and because they could be a key to deeper understanding of the new system.

The sources of these variations seem to be different from anything occurring before the change – there is no gradual build-up or tapering off. If these temporary upsurges are excluded, the contrast in variability between before and after is even more striking. The wave-like variations in tension before the change can be reasonably interpreted as a function of staff–inmate relations, i.e. as due to the inherent instability of the staff–inmate relation, with consequent accumulation of tension and its gradual dissipation, once a certain level is reached. Similarly, the smoother curve that exists for most of the after period seems to reflect more stable staff–inmate relations. The upsurges bear no such obvious relation but rather suggest, because of the suddenness of their onset and the speed of recovery, a temporary upset due to forces arising from outside the immediate officer–inmate relation. The apparent periodicity suggests that the source is nevertheless within the system and not 'accidental' (e.g. transfers from other prisons). Examination of the incidents occurring at these points shows that each upsurge corresponds to an order from above to 'tighten up' some aspects of discipline. These recurrent campaigns were mainly directed at cleanliness of cells, use of toilets at the end of association, and attendance at classes. They were at least in part an attempt to solve organizational difficulties arising from the introduction of association, e.g. the shorter time spent in cells created a relative shortage of buckets and other cleaning equipment (there being less chance of staggering the times of use). It was some time before the end of association was consistently defined and a preliminary warning instituted that would prepare the inmates for breaking up of games, using the toilet, and moving to cells. The half-hour overlap of educational classes and association created what was, in the eyes of the inmates, an unnecessary conflict situation.

Whatever the justification of these campaigns, the significant feature for staff–inmate relations was that they were initiated from above. The disciplinary officers themselves appeared to be more desirous of remedying the causes than of simply suppressing the symptoms. This would explain why there was no prior process of build-up in tension, and why (bearing in mind that the attitude of the disciplinary officers was communicated to the inmates) there was a quick return to normality without a significant carryover of hostility.

It is a moot point whether such intervention (with the corresponding eruption of tension) is likely to upset staff–inmate relations to such an extent that they fail to return to the previous constant level. The clear danger is that the basic-grade staff will feel these campaigns to be an unjustified reflection upon their performance. This could generate staff–management tension and lead even those officers previously most active in controlling the inmates to withdraw from their roles.

From the point of view of those in charge of the prison, this does suggest the need to manage as far as possible by manipulating the conditions determining staff–inmate relations rather than by direct intervention.

(c) *A greater stability in the face of external changes.* Pertinent evidence of the stability of officer–inmate relations after the change is the apparent insensitivity of these relations to changes in the size of the inmate population. Where living-space is as restricted as in Bristol Prison during the whole of this period, an increase in population brings about not only new social relations but also increased interpersonal friction. Little is known of these ecological effects on human behaviour, but in Bristol Prison the ratio of population to living-space was such that any increase meant more than three men to a cell (designed for one), more men using very limited toilet facilities at the same time, more crowding on the staircases and in the passageways, and more men literally elbow to elbow in their work-places. These things, while incidental in themselves, together constitute an increase in interpersonal friction which, in the general absence of positive sentiments between inmates, is likely to generate tension. Before the change, an increase in population did correspond with an increase in the level of tension (τ correlation $= + 0.42$, $0.10 > p > .05$), but no such relation is observable after ($\tau = .03$). The multitude of minor inconveniences and irritations that accompany population change when space is short added to the overt conflict before the change but are tolerated afterwards.

It may be that this change is due to a lessening of the effects of crowding on cell life (less time being spent in cells) or a greater tolerance of the inmates for the frustrations of crowding. It is unlikely that it is simply due to a sort of threshold effect such that 'beyond a certain population size a few extra make no difference'. The range of population size after the change overlaps considerably with the range before, and consequently any such 'threshold effect' would either have been observed before the change or, at the most, have produced a lower positive correlation after; one would not expect such a threshold effect to produce an absence of correlation. Either of the two likely explanations suggests greater stability.

(d) *Smaller differences in staff and inmate attitudes.* Some support for the above evidence of the increased stability in staff–inmate relations is given by the attitudes of the core samples before and after change. There is, first, an increased similarity in their views about the value of association for the inmates.

Table 19 – Staff and inmates' assessment of the value* of association for the inmates

	Before		After	
	Inmates	*Staff*	*Inmates*	*Staff*
Positive	14	6	27	18
Doubtful	12	5	2	2
Negative	4	9	1	—

*Whereas inmates tended to assume that their fellows would like what was of value to them, the staff made a clear distinction. Hence the staff answers are different from those given when asked whether they thought inmates would like association.

In so far as association has become a key feature of prison life, agreement on this matter would tend to lessen misunderstanding and conflict. Much less hostility and mistrust is also found in the beliefs of the staff and inmates about the amount of cooperation that each group could expect from the other.

Before the change, each party agreed that the members of the other were the sort of men who could not be trusted and who would be spiteful and uncooperative. After the change, each had a higher opinion of the other.

This increase in mutual trust would, if common to other inmates and staff, make relations more stable. In the event of an incident, there would be less tendency to jump to the conclusion that the inmate was 'trying to get away with something' or the officer 'trying to have a go at one'. Both parties would be more likely to consider

Table 20 – Staff and inmates attitudes to each other's behaviour

| | Expected before | | Believed after | |
	By inmates of staff	By staff of inmates	By inmates of staff	By staff of inmates
Helpful or cooperative	4	6	16	15
Doubtful or uninterested	11	9	9	4
Uncooperative	15	5	5	1
	30	20	30	20

the incident on its own merit without allowing it to spill over into other matters.

At the same time, the public and private attitudes of the staff shifted toward a more favourable view of the scheme.

Over half of the doubtful and unfavourable attitudes attributed to

Table 21 – Public and private attitudes of staff to the new system (as seen by officers)

| | Before (July 1958) | | After (Dec. 1958) | |
	Own attitudes	Attitudes attributed to staff as a whole	Own attitudes	Attitudes attributed to staff as a whole
Favour association	8	0	12	9
Doubtful	3	3	2	10
Prefer old system	9	17	6	1
	20	20	20	20

the staff as a whole are put down to the additional burden of duties, etc., not to a dislike of association *per se*.

If this is taken into account, it is clear that a more pronounced shift has taken place in public attitudes than in private ones. Bearing in mind the earlier evidence on private beliefs and attitudes of the staff, it does seem that a substantial minority, while admitting the value of the scheme for inmates, feels that it fails to meet their ideas of what a prison is for and their own needs for respect and power. Some sense of their attitudes can be gleaned from the following statements made by this minority after the change:

'Prison should be a deterrent – I prefer the old system, and so would the public.' (Officer 1.)
'The place should be for punishment.' (Officer 2.)
'I am only interested in more responsibility being given to the officer.' (Officer 3.)
'There is now too little respect for the officer.' (Officer 4.)
'There is too little security and too much laxness for me – too many of the other officers are getting lax.' (Officer 5.)

However, these officers, with one exception, recognize the discrepancy between their private attitude and the public staff attitude of tolerance and even approval for the scheme. This has been brought home to several of them by informal incidents in which other officers have point-blank refused to help them persecute some prisoner – although such joint staff pursuits were previously not unknown.

The inmates appear to be quite conscious of this change. Whereas in the June and July interviews, they condemned the staff as a whole and regarded the 'good, fair' officer as the exception; after the change, it was the 'bad, unfair' officer who was so regarded. Discussion with inmates of incidents occurring after the change, in which they had been involved with this particular minority of officers, revealed the extent of the change. With few exceptions, any remaining sense of hostility was directed at the particular officer concerned and not, as was normal before, generalized to the staff and Bristol Prison as a whole.

There is another side to this increased interaction of inmates and their increased openness to outside influence. It is not unknown in the history of penology (or in many present establishments, if some of these inmates are to be believed) that such conditions lead to the spread and enrichment of a criminal culture. One cannot say for certain that this has not in fact occurred at Bristol, but several convergent lines of evidence suggest not.

As already pointed out, there was a high level of active participation in games during association, and no evidence of any significant minority persistently huddled in furtive conversation. It is not

G

difficult to detect if a group in a public setting is engaged in discussing matters they would not like others to hear. Walking repeatedly around the Bristol association, the author only rarely detected any sign of such conversations going on between more than two inmates (not unnaturally, they were common between pairs); more frequently, there would be an overt invitation or some gesture or action to indicate that it was all right to sit in. With the rotation of duties, nearly every officer in the sample had had ample opportunity to do association duty. Their observations, sharpened by experience and immediate concern for security that the author did not possess, support the above evidence. Before the change there was a strong body of officer opinion that the greater freedom of association would enable the growth in power of informal inmate society with an emphasis upon criminal values and a strengthening of the influence of 'barons' and 'toughs'. Despite this expectation, their judgement after experiencing the new system was that no substantial change had taken place. Some officers, as well as some inmates, drew a sharp contrast in this matter with the old small association of long-term prisoners waiting to be sent on to Central Prisons.

Table 22 – The influence of 'barons' and 'toughs' (as seen by officers)

	Expectations before	Judgement after
Increased influence	10	1
No less, no more	9	17
Decreased influence	1	2

The following extracts indicate the bases of judgement:

'They are still lively but no increase in their power.' (Officer 6.)
'Some signs at first of gangs, but now O.K.' (Officer 7.)
'Surprisingly enough, the barons haven't tried to make hay.' (Officer 8.)
'Borrowing was already becoming less of a problem and certainly hasn't got worse.' (Officer 9.)

From a number of persons who had reasons to believe that confidences would be kept, it was possible to reconstruct and cross-check an elementary picture back to early June 1958 of the major gambling activities, the persons involved, the financial trends, and the sanctions meted out (including those not officially observed and reported). The impression gained was that the course of this activity was independent of, and not particularly affected one way or another by, association. This does not exclude the possibility that with different kinds of inmates controlling the 'books' they might seek to exploit the opportunities provided by association. One cannot tell whether the new level of mutual support between inmates could withstand such an attempt.

Thus, under the prevailing conditions, the evidence is that there has been no noticeable increase in inmate corruption or exploitation.

Prediction 4: Other effects on the inmates of 'A' Hall

(a) 'That the inmate will tend to be less centred on himself or his relation with officers and more drawn out into participation with others.'

It was also implicit in the earlier discussion of what was expected from the change that:

(b) 'The inmates would be generally more open to what was going on outside their immediate affairs.'

The first part of the prediction is substantially supported by the evidence presented earlier on the active participation in association. Some slight additional evidence is provided by the data on inmates' friendships gathered from the sample of inmates and checked against staff observations. These two sets of data tallied almost precisely, suggesting that in a prison of this size one may conceal what one does but not with whom one does it.

Table 23 – Friendships between inmates in the sample ($n = 30$)

	Before (*July 1958*)	After (*Dec. 1958*)
Number linked by reciprocal choice	4	10
Number chosen but not reciprocating	2	4

It is doubtful whether the tendencies shown in *Table 23* can be put down simply to the fact that these men have been together six months longer at the time of the second measure. The majority firmly believed in July that they had all the friends they needed, and their stated friendships and staff observations suggested that they did seem to be following policies established during earlier prison experience. More clear-cut than the increase in number of close friendships is the general agreement after the change that they were on nodding terms or even friendly with a great many more inmates than they ever expected to be in this prison.

The second part of this prediction brings us as near to the problem of rehabilitation and reform as the study comes. Although it was not technically possible to set the questions of whether the changes would reform more of the inmates, it is feasible to ask whether the changes have produced conditions more likely to aid or to hinder reform.

Reduction of the general level of tension and of the personal antagonisms between officers and inmates alone could be expected to reduce the tendency of inmates to protect themselves by withdrawing into their cells and their own phantasies. Before the change, eighteen of the inmates in the sample felt that they would probably be better off if they stayed behind cell doors than if they went out on association. After the change, only seven preferred to stay in; and only three of these felt that, in general, the cell was better than association. In discussion of the problem of adjustment that they had faced after earlier prison sentences, all but three of the inmates (and these three generally lacked insight) made some spontaneous mention of feeling unsure and retiring in situations demanding simple social intercourse. Some, of course, put this forward as a general observation they had made of other ex-prisoners, not of themselves. This was a common observation in Bristol Prison; it was also made by diverse members of the staff and even appeared in the records. There is thus some reason for believing that the conditions after change are less likely to create the sort of cell mentality – a generalized withdrawal from social relations – that in itself hinders rehabilitation.

Similarly, the conditions after change seemed to engender less of an atmosphere of fear, hostility, and suspicion between inmates and staff. One would expect as a result that lengthy confinement would be less likely to create such an attitude to authority in general.

Beyond these general observations, it is useful to consider some of the specific, though peripheral, data that are available. Practically every inmate interviewed spoke of association as helping him or the others to 'get out of themselves'. Even if this is accepted, the question still arises as to whether association is simply a new and better escape. If it is, one should expect to find a decline in the other activities normally serving to get a man out of his cell or to take his mind off his confinement. Attendance at educational classes, reading books or newspapers, and writing letters are activities that in part serve this function and are important to the administration as manifestations of their desire to aid the reform of the individual.[1]

Attendance at educational classes is only partly controlled by administrative rules, but there is no overall consistent decline in the monthly enrolment figures or in the actual attendances that can be put down to the change. Discussion of their class enrolments and attendance records with the inmate sample suggest that, but for administrative pressure, their attendance would have been lower. The most frequent reason was that, despite their interest in the classes they had chosen, they were unwilling to cut into their evening association by going off early to classes.

Use of the library increased consistently over the whole period of study (special requests for books rising to just on fifty per weekday), but it is likely that this was due largely to improved library services, not to any effects arising from the change. According to the inmate sample they read less than before, but still took as many books (with one exception who said he read more because he could now keep his mind on his book).

Even allowing for the increase in population and the availability of free newspapers on association, the number of newspapers circulating increased steadily at least during the first six months after the change. In this case, the change may have been a function of the increased freedom for discussion between inmates. Canteen letters were the only other item of this kind on which data were collected. In so far as these have to be paid for by inmates, it was thought that they would provide a simple, if gross, indicator of the overall level of concern with family and friends on the outside. The average rate of purchase dropped from 13·3 per hundred inmates before the change to 11·0 per hundred for the first six months after. The old rate was then recovered, averaging 13·7 for the second six months.

There is nothing in the above data to indicate a major substitution of association for other activities. Even the temporary decline in the

---

[1] Attendance at religious services is so tied up with the administrative rules that it provides no index of the effects of the change.

rate of purchasing canteen letters might indicate no more than that inmates felt less need to solicit sympathy from outside friends and kin. Where there are instances of withdrawal from other activities, these seem to represent a simple conflict of interests. At the same time, the data do not provide any unambiguous evidence of an extension of interests. Some specially constructed test would probably be required to answer this problem.

THE MAJOR EFFECTS OBSERVED IN 'D' HALL

'D' Hall was not studied in the same detail or over as long a period as 'A' Hall on the grounds that it is not the main problem of the Local Prison. Nevertheless, it is not negligible and in this instance provides some check on the main results observed in 'A' Hall.

One of the first points of difference is that there was no extended period of transitional readjustment in 'D' Hall.

Figure 7   Half-hourly distribution of offences in 'D' Hall

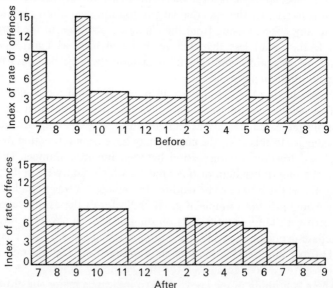

The Effect of Increased Opportunities for Offending

As the following graph shows, there is again no evidence for assuming that an increase in freedom of association must lead to an increase in the number of incidents.

Despite the introduction of association, there was no increase in the rate of offences during these hours, and there was a decline in the rate of offences during exercise and in the evening. The restlessness that formerly characterized 'D' wing of an evening practically disappeared.

The General Level of Tension

(a) The total number of offences declined after the change. For the eight consecutive four-weekly periods before the change, the mean numbers of incidents was 15·9 and only 9·4 for the twelve four-weekly periods after the change ($z = 1·97$, $p = 0·05$). In terms of offences/1000 man-days, the rate declined from 4·66 to 2·74 ($z = 3·05$, $p < 0·01$). Thus, if incidents had occurred at the same rate as before, one would have expected 189 – 70 per cent more than actually reported.

(b) Unlike 'A' Hall, the decline in offences extended to a certain degree to the work situation.

Table 24 – Mean rate of disciplinary offences/four-week period

	Before (*8 periods*)	*After* (*12 periods*)	*Significance of the difference*
Domestic sector	9·9	6·0	$z = 4·52$: $p < 0·001$
Work sector	6·0	3·25	$z = 1·97$: $p = 0·05$

(c) Incidents involving threatening or abuse of an officer occur less frequently than in 'A' Hall and, although they decrease after the change, this is not statistically significant.

Table 25 – Changes in rate of occurrence of incidents involving verbal or other attacks on officers

	Mean rate		
	Before	*After*	*Significance*
Domestic sector	2·37	1·17	n.s.
Work sector	1·12	0·50	n.s.

(d) As in 'A' Hall, the effects of the change were most marked among the younger inmates.

These changes cannot, however, be divorced from the steps that were taken in 'D' Hall to provide a special association for the boys.

Stability of the Officer–Inmate Relation

Two sets of data suggest that the changes also produced greater stability in 'D' Hall.

Table 26 – Contribution to total number of offences made by Borstal Trainees and Young Prisoners (including Y P awaiting trial)

	% BTs & YPs in 'D' Hall population	% of all offences that are due to BTs & YPs	Index of over-contribution to total offences*	Significance of reduction after change
Non-work				
Before transition	15·5	55·5	$\chi^2 = 40·5$	
After transition	17·0	30·0	16·9	$\chi^2 = 9·65$ $p < 0·01$
Work				
Before transition		43·0	25·7	
After transition		32·6	9·6	$\chi^2 = 3·96$ $0·10 > p > 0·05$

(*All the values of χ^2 in this column are significant at least at the one per cent level.)

First, an examination of the distribution of offences per week showed that, before the change, it differed significantly from a Poisson distribution, but after the change, it did not.

Second, the level of tension after the change was found to be insensitive to variations in the size of the BT and YP group. In 'D' Hall there is no correlation between total population and offences. However, there is a high correlation between BTs and YPs and offences. ($\tau = 0·56$, $p = ·02$; for the sign test $p < ·001$.) After the change there is zero correlation ($\tau = 0·048$).

Overall, 'D' Hall appears to show the same kinds of effects as

Table 27 – Approximation to Poisson distribution of offences/week

		'D' Hall	
		Non-work	Work
	x^2	20·90	7·45
Before			
(8 periods)	df.	4	2
	$p <$	·001	·05
	x^2	2·58	3·96
After			
(8 periods)	df.	3	2
	$p <$	n.s.	n.s.

observed in 'A' Hall. It apparently differs in readiness to change (e.g. the quicker transition and the spread of effect to the work situation) and shows least change in an aspect in which it is already quite different – verbal and other attacks on officers.

5 · Results of the experiment and the new dilemmas

Care was taken in the preceding pages to make explicit theoretical notions and practical procedures and considerations that entered into the design and study of this experiment. The attempt to cover all these pros and cons has been guided by an awareness that this was a field experiment, with all of the usual lack of control over relevant variables and with the additional difficulty that there was, on my own part, considerable doubt as to what these were.

In presenting the evidence, greatest weight was placed upon measures of modes of behaviour continuously generated within ordinary prison life and publicly recorded. These are the kinds of behaviour that in other such prisons offer the best guide to administrative action. In the same way, the various kinds of evidence were focused on those five issues which I judged to be keys for interpreting the study and for drawing conclusions of administrative significance. The evidence on these issues was as follows:

(a) The steps taken at Bristol successfully created an association that was attractive to the inmates and involved the majority of the participants in active leisure pursuits.

(b) The observed effects of these changes were irreconcilable with any assumption that the unruliness of the inmate population (and hence the general level of tension) was simply a function of its propensity to act criminally and of the opportunities to do so.

(c) The general level of tension was reduced. The areas of prison life and the inmates in which this reduction were most marked were those predicted by assuming that the level of tension was primarily a function of the relative deprivation of inmates, i.e. in the domestic sector and with the younger inmates.[1]

[1] Initially it was thought on more psychological grounds that different kinds of inmates might react differently to association. Each case was classified according to his major reference group – criminal, prisoner's family, etc. – and according to his degree of institutionalization. Neither of these classifications

(d) The introduction of association resolved the instability that had hitherto appeared to be inherent in the relations between basic-grade disciplinary officers and inmates. With this went a significant decline in inmate hostility to officers, a lessening of mutual distrust, and the virtual disappearance of the schism in the officer ranks between 'activists' and 'passengers'.

(e) In some important respects, the experiment appears to have created the grounds on which reformative and rehabilitative efforts with the inmates might more successfully be pursued. In particular, there was less tendency for inmates to develop a prison mentality or to become more bitter or antagonistic towards authority in general.

In summary, the introduction of association into Bristol Prison appears to have produced significant changes in the behaviour and attitudes of staff and inmates. These changes have been in the planned direction.

Introduction of association has not had the effect simply of moving Bristol from a state of disequilibrium to one of equilibrium. It has had the effect of resolving wholly or in part some of the earlier problems and bringing forward or creating a set of new ones. Some of these new problems can be more or less clearly defined. They may be classified as follows:

(a) *Problems of supporting the existing system in operation*

    (i) One is particularly impressed with the fact that association is not a self-sustaining form of social life. Some external supports and controls are probably necessary if association is not to become less active and less attractive. Measures taken at Bristol included the establishment of chess classes that served to feed a stream of chess enthusiasts into the association, and games competitions that were run by the inmates for six weeks before Christmas. It would seem that additional measures should always be

---

correlated with the observed differences in individual reactions to the change. Re-analysis was made of the cases in the sample who wanted to be off association or who were on association because of their friends but felt that the change was no improvement. The numbers were few, but the evidence is that these men differed from the majority in the extent of either their psychopathic tendencies or their neuroses.

under consideration. The class of appropriate measures would not seem to include the formation of standing inmate committees. An inmate committee to organize competitions is one thing – it has a specific and concrete brief and ceases to exist when this is carried out. A standing committee is another because, even if its brief is formally restricted, its continuity is an encouragement to inmate self-government and to the emergence of inmate leaders who owe their popularity to their militancy. The assumptions of a closed prison imply that every step should be taken to inhibit the growth of inmate self-government.

The above-mentioned measures are, it will be noted, all directed toward supporting or enriching the freely chosen and enacted inmate leisure-time. Any outside interference in what is to be played and when might well change the character and value of the association.

(ii) The question of staff conditions cannot be entirely divorced from measures taken to improve the lot of the inmates. As we had occasion to note during the course of this study, the staff are particularly apt to compare their treatment by the Commissioners with that given to the inmates. This issue comes sharply to the fore when, as in this case, providing better conditions for the inmates throws an extra burden of duties on the staff. In the absence of criteria of staff-load that are operationally defined and administratively efficient, the staff find themselves in a position where, while the inmates have got benefits without asking, their own 'just requests' for additional staff or payment instead of time in lieu for additional duties appear to be neither appreciated nor understood. In the handling of local matters, there needs to be sufficient flexibility in the interpretation of standing orders to convince the staff that their problems are being sympathetically considered in the light of the new conditions.

(b) *Those problems concerned with removing the limits on the spread of effect from the association*

Foremost in this category is the question of work. It did seem that the work situation had become increasingly anachronistic in the eyes of the inmates. The nature of the tasks, the system of payment, and the social relations on the job all stand in contrast to the conditions created in the domestic sector of prison life. One might even predict that unless this situation is remedied, it would tend to get worse, not just remain as it is.

(c) *Those problems concerned with taking advantage of the gains already made in order to further the attainment of the purpose of the prison service*

Two problems are apparent here:

   (i) It is necessary to think about strengthening and clarifying the senior executive roles inside the prison. There was some evidence that a new source of instability had emerged somewhere in the relations between the senior officers and those in basic disciplinary roles.

   During the period of changing over to the new system, the governor must inevitably involve himself in a great many of the details of internal prison life. When the new system is established, this seems to be neither necessary nor desirable; it becomes possible for the governor to manage his prison by means of his inspectorial and judicial functions and by his control or influence over the 'boundary conditions'. The boundary conditions in this case are in particular the kind of staff and inmates entering and leaving, the welfare provisions for inmates, and the locally determined aspects of staff employment. By managing these matters, the governor can make the job of the officers and the life of the inmates less frustrating. In order to strengthen the hand of the governor in these matters, it would seem advisable to bring the prison psychologist and the welfare officer[1] under his immediate command. Within this framework, the chief officer would be expected to manage the routine internal problems.

[1] There is a case for an assistant governor II having responsibility for the welfare function (and reception and discharge of inmates) so that decisions made in this area are made not only at the appropriate level but with full cognizance of the requirements of security and good order. This would be valuable training for the role of governor suggested above, provided, of course, that the initial training of assistant governors had thoroughly indoctrinated them in the primacy of security and good order.

It is my feeling that something might have to be done to clarify the relation between the governor and his chief officers and at the same time to strengthen the governor's role by bringing into his immediate command group such staff as would enable him to control and provide for welfare and similar functions.

(ii) There should be some reconsideration of the other aspect of the Norwich scheme – the redefinition of the disciplinary officer's role to include a counselling component. Two aspects of this proposal may be distinguished. The first, the writing of reports on the personality of the inmates does not necessarily involve counselling in the full sense of the word. There is, however, little to be said in favour of report-writing if done without any special knowledge of the inmates concerned. Without such knowledge and in the absence of psychological training in making and communicating judgements of personality, the reporting must remain at the level at which, for instance, selection of red-bands (trusties) occurs. Counselling is the more serious proposition.

Despite the improvement in staff–inmate relations that has taken place at Bristol (steadily maintained up to the last observations in September 1960), it is still not possible to recommend any change in the disciplinary officer's role. That role has become more manageable because it is easier to maintain a certain distance from the inmate and his personal life. It is no longer so important to be either feared or liked by inmates. Instructing the officers to build up personal relations with the inmates with a view to helping them with their personal problems would, if acted upon, tend to undermine the present achievement. Probably many officers could overcome the implications of superiority and inferiority that are inherent in one-way helping and develop personal relations with the inmates. Fewer could provide the sort of psychological help that usually requires professionally trained counsellors. (Material help must for the most part be reserved for the welfare officers and others who can enter into relations with an inmate's kin, previous employer, etc.) Only a small minority could do all of this and at the same time hold themselves sufficiently above their feelings of sympathy and friendliness to the inmate to observe the primary tasks of their role – the maintenance of security and good order.[1]

As shown by Grusky's study of a small Californian prison camp,[2] the effects of combining in the basic-grade role the psychologically contradictory tasks of prison warder and counsellor would be the emergence of a new schism in the staff – counsellor-oriented versus discipline-oriented – and a loss of morale in the disciplinarians as they find their attempts to maintain security and order undermined by fellow-officers bent on the reform of their charges.

This is not to say that counselling is unnecessary in the local prison. With the changes that have taken place, it is no longer necessary for the staff to 'screw down' on the inmates and they are prepared to let other agencies have access to their charges – provided such access is used to aid their task of maintaining security and order and not to subvert it. In particular, they are prepared to recognize that their task would be helped by any procedure for identifying and reallocating (if they cannot be helped by local professionals) that small element of neurotics and aggressive psychopaths who fail to respond to the prevailing conditions.

After trying for two and a half years to understand how a single prison worked and relating this to published American efforts, I am of the belief that the following propositions may still be asserted as a reasonable challenge to other social scientists and a caution to those who have to operate prison systems in the 'here and now':

---

[1] The psychological difficulties of offering help in the staff–inmate relation are readily understood in terms of general discussion. (See Heider, F. *Psychology of Interpersonal Relations,* New York, Wiley, 1958; and Ladieu, G., Hanfmann, E., and Dembo, T. 'Studies in Adjustment to Visible Injuries: Evaluation of Help by the Injured', *J. abnorm. soc. Psychol.,* 1947, **42**, 169.)

[2] Grusky, O. 'Role Conflict in Organization: A Study of Prison Camp Officials', *Admin. Sci. Quart.,* 1959, **3**, 452–472.

(a) Given the requirement of medium or maximum security,[1] the prison regime cannot be expected to be a reformative agent.

(b) Given the requirement of security, a level of internal freedom cannot be found that will automatically secure good order. Supervision and coercion will be necessary.

(c) Given the requirements of security and good order, the role of the ordinary officer cannot be defined as that of also being the prisoner's friend and counsellor.

These propositions have been formulated as bluntly as possible in order to command attention even at the risk of inviting immediate unfavourable reactions. The issues they raise have been central to social-scientific studies of prisons.[2] They are also important to the leadership of prison institutions because setting goals too high will lead to inefficient allocation of resources and loss of control over the behaviour of those expected to pursue such goals in daily practice. On the other hand, setting goals too low is likely to cause unnecessary costs to outside bodies and also waste the resources allocated to the system.

The first proposition is the key one. It should be noted that it derives from the observations of what happens when the requirement that there shall be no escape is translated into daily practice. In the first chapter we tried to outline these processes. The changes made in the Bristol prison seem to have taken the steam out of some of these processes but it did not change the fact that for the prisoners (excluding a few for whom prison was a refuge) the enforcement of security was a constant pressure which continued to give adaptive meaning to the folkways and mores of prison culture. There was less fear of getting into the bad books of particular officers and more willingness to accept that the officers were just doing their job. There was no noticeable change in the belief that this job was to watch them, anticipate their moves, and apprehend them for breaches of

---

[1] Rather more attention ought to be given to the relation between the cost of security and the losses incurred through lack of security. The costs of security not only are financial, but also include a loss of rehabilitative possibilities; the losses incurred by the community are not the same for a petty thief as for a psychopathic killer. It may be that an optimum balance can only be achieved by provision of a wider range of secure places.

[2] See Mathiesen, T. 'The Sociology of Prisons: Problems for Future Research,' *Brit. J. Sociol.*, 1966, **17**, 360–379.

the regulations. The lessening of antagonism to the values of the institution did not seemingly imply an increase in identification with these values. For the inmates, Bristol was still a prison not an educational or productive institution. Officers as a class were still antagonists not teachers.

I have suggested by my wording that the level of security is a key determinant of what can be done to create an atmosphere where character reform is accepted by the inmates as a pervading purpose of the institution (regardless of whether they actually change). It is, however, a moot point whether therapeutic techniques are as yet effective, even in an open prison. All that I am arguing is that if we feel that we have to have the security afforded by the medium and maximum security prisons, then we should accept that these will be custodial institutions not reformative institutions, and that certain other costs will be unavoidable. This is not to deny the importance of striving, as in this experiment, to eliminate self-defeating repression and of facilitating the operation of potentially reformative influences such as outside contacts, prison visitors, education and welfare workers.

H

Appendix I · Outline of a study of the effects of adopting the 'Norwich' system in the Bristol Local Prison

THE MAIN PHASES OF THE STUDY

1. *Visits to Winchester, Lincoln, and Leicester Local Prisons* to get a background knowledge of this type of prison (1, 7, and 9 May respectively).

2. *Visit to Norwich Local Prison.* We have been given to understand that the main features of the new Norwich system are keeping prisoners in association throughout the day, allocating the minding of groups of prisoners (about eight in each group) to specific officers, and the pairing of officers. If the design of the Bristol study is to be reasonably efficient we will need further information about the Norwich experiment.

3. It is expected that discussions and observations at Norwich will help us to understand:
   (a) the effects originally sought by introducing the changes;
   (b) how these changes were introduced and initially received by the staff and inmates;
   (c) what changes have subsequently been manifested in prisoner behaviour, within prison and after leaving, between prisoners and staff, within the staff;
   (d) what further innovations are being considered as desirable or necessary.

4. Furthermore, it will be necessary to discuss the experiences they have had with imparting their methods to Oxford and Shrewsbury and their intentions with regard to Bristol.
   (Estimated field-time – 5 days)

6. *Study of Bristol before the changes are introduced.* To get a baseline for measuring the effects of the change, it will be necessary

to make a study of the conditions already existing in the prison. Attention will be focused on those aspects found to be persistent in a prison such as Bristol is at present, and shown to be affected by the changes introduced at Norwich. On our present information it would seem that the important problems include:

(a) changes in the orientation of prisoners toward the 'outside';
(b) the extent and quality of relations between the prisoners, the prisoners and the staff, and between the staff members;
(c) the general level of tension

(Estimated field-time – 3 weeks)

7. *Formulation of the specific steps needed to introduce the Norwich system.* The TIHR research worker will take part in the discussions between the governor and his staff about the steps needed to introduce the Norwich system at Bristol. The first task will be to make a thorough appreciation of the Norwich, Oxford, and Shrewsbury experience and

(a) to consider how to transmit these experiences to the Bristol staff; and
(b) to plan the selection, preparation, and subsequent utilization of staff to go to Norwich.

8. The results of the considerations of the governor and of the TIHR will be presented to a meeting at headquarters towards the end of June. At this meeting, Norwich and the TIHR Management Committee should be represented.

9. *Visit to Norwich with the Bristol staff* early in July in order to see the kinds of changes induced and the queries that arise, and to consider what modifications might usefully be made to future visits of this kind.

(Field-time dependent upon decisions of the governor)

10. *Study of the planning of the changes to be introduced in Bristol.* A close study of the changes proposed and the manner in which they are planned and introduced will be necessary if the subsequent effects are to be validly interpreted. It is most desirable that the intended changes be explicitly formulated, and their introduction planned in some detail. In the absence of such

planning, it will be rather difficult to determine to what any of the observed effects refer.

11. These plans might be presented to a Headquarters meeting of the sort mentioned above, in time for a start to be made during July.

12. *Study of the introduction of the changes.* An intensive study will be needed of these changes, as it is unlikely that they will conform exactly to plan. A knowledge of the manner and order in which the changes are carried out should throw considerable light on the nature of the prison community and will be invaluable in interpreting the observed effects. It should be possible to introduce the changes in September.
(Field-time dependent upon the plan adopted by the governor)

13. *Study of the effects of the changes.* Some time after the changes have been introduced and after there has been some settling down, e.g. three to four months, it will be necessary to collect data that are comparable with those collected beforehand. It will be necessary to repeat these 'after-measures' several months later, in order to get some indication of the stability of the changes and, in particular, the extent to which the changes are effective with inmates who enter prison for the first time after the changes have been established.

14. During this phase, special attention will be given to those unintended and unobserved processes set in motion by the changes as well as those intended or obvious. (As examples of what is referred to here, one may mention that the Norwich system might possibly encourage immature dependency on the part of certain types of inmates. It might increase the power and influence of the informal cliques of the prisoners at the expense of that of the officers, or it might make impossible demands on certain types of officers.)
(Estimated field-time for the study of
effects – three weeks on each occasion)

15. The final report will need to be worked through with the gover-

nor, considered by his working party, and presented to a meeting at headquarters early next year. In keeping with the policy of the TIHR, there will be no publication of results without these being first cleared with the Commissioners.

16. The report will cover the description and analysis of the nine phases and, in addition, indicate some of the questions that are left unanswered.

THE KIND OF INFORMATION TO BE COLLECTED

17. Three main kinds of information will be sought:
    (a) that which will enable a precise description of the social structure brought about by introducing the Norwich-type system.
    (b) facts which will test hypotheses about the effects of the changes. These will include evidence of changes in roles, in informal social relations, and general level of tension.
    (c) facts which will permit a description of the psychological processes set in motion by the changes. In particular, evidence will be sought of changes in the way the prison is seen by staff and inmates, and of changes in their needs and in their modes of adjustment to prison life.

SOME PROBLEMS OF COLLECTING INFORMATION

18. It is not considered that any particular problem will be encountered in the collection of information about the social structure. Granted the cooperation of the institution, this sort of information is usually obtainable by interviews with individuals and groups who are strategically placed with regard to knowing how the institution operates. Some systematic observations will be made in order to make the research worker aware of those things that are 'obvious' to persons in constant contact with the prison. This latter may involve attachment to selected officers for a shift as well as some repeated observation of the major recurrent events in the prison life.

19. Information about changes in roles, social relations, and level of tension may include:

(a) records of the kind customarily kept by the staff;

(b) some systematic observations by the research worker, and possibly by selected staff members, for the specific purposes of this study; and

(c) interviews with selected staff and inmates.

These interviews may be mostly with groups, since much of the required information of this type concerns common and shared reactions. However, some of the information will have to be sought in the individual interviews concerned with the third type of information. All interviews will depend upon the voluntary cooperation of the staff or prisoners concerned.

20. Individual interviews with a representative sample of inmates and staff will be required for direct evidence of psychological processes. This involves rather complex problems of sampling, and no final decision can be made before the first visit to Bristol. The prison inmates are so varied that it probably will not be possible to measure with any reliability the effect on all the different types. On our present information, the prison population of Bristol at the time of studying the 'before change' situation might be classified as follows:

Those who will have left before the after measurement'

{
Released (including practically all with less than six months) (1)

Transferred to 'open' (all) (2)

to 'correctives' (all) (3)

to 'closed' (4)
}

Those who are likely still to be present

{
Serving time there and not yet released (those with more than six months) (5)

Many of those waiting for transfer to closed prisons (6)
}

It is expected that information will be available at Bristol to permit a sample design that will take into account factors of this kind.

21. Thus, before and after measures of the behaviour of the same

person only seem feasible for sub-groups 5 and 6, i.e. those sentenced to serve at least six months in Bristol and those waiting for transfer to closed prisons. Among those is likely to be a large proportion of recidivists and a few of the hopefuls. Before and after measures of the same person give so much additional information that it is planned to select a single random sample from sub-groups 5 and 6 and use this on each occasion.

22. A separate sample will have to be drawn from the other strata (sub-groups 1–4) for each occasion. In their case, some matching may be possible.

23. Emphasis is being placed upon interviewing because the prison situation seems unsuited to the extensive use of paper-and-pencil questionnaires and tests. This places severe restrictions upon the size of the sample that can be handled, probably keeping it within the range of 36–50. These randomly sampled interviews, however, do not constitute the only, or even necessarily the most important, source of evidence.

Appendix II · Methodological notes

1. SAMPLING OF INMATES AND OFFICERS

The inmate sample was selected by means of a table of random numbers from all ordinary-class inmates of 'A' Hall who were already in prison in June 1958, and whose sentences would not be served before 1 January 1959. The only men excluded were those on the verge of transfer to Central Prisons.

Inmate sample

Strata	Numbers present and not out before 1.1.59	Number randomly selected	Planned sampling ratio	Loss
Sentence under 3 years	56	16	1 : 3·5	—
Sentence over 3 years	45	16	1 : 2·8	2
	101	32		2

Two cases were transferred between June and February, reducing the sample for purposes of comparison to thirty.

The sample of disciplinary officers was also selected by means of a table of random numbers. Before selection, those officers were eliminated who had only joined the Bristol staff in 1958, were within five years of retirement for age, or were frequently absent on sick leave. Two-thirds of the remaining list was selected and, with the loss of two due to transfers, the sample for before-after comparisons was twenty.

2. ADDITIONAL INTERVIEWS

Apart from the sample, interviews were also held, during each period of field study, with the persons officially occupying key staff and inmate positions and with a small number of staff and inmates who occupied no special position, but with whom the author had frequent contact.

The first group provided a necessary source of sociologically relevant data and the latter repeatedly hoped to suggest new aspects of incidents and trends being investigated.

All but four of the staff not included in the sample, or the other two groups, were casually interviewed while at their post or in the officers' mess. These casual interviews were focused upon attitudes and beliefs about the prison system. Background information frequently emerged but was not systematically sought in these cases and hence not systematically analysed.

3. OBSERVATIONS

A crude sampling procedure for observations was operated during each period of field study. A list was made out beforehand of the main phases and places of activity throughout the day, and a timetable laid down to give an irregular pattern of repeated visits. The timetable was modified to meet current contingencies, but the frequency and irregularity were maintained. The irregularity was intended to lessen any effects due to anticipation by staff or inmates of being visited.

The knowledge on the part of staff and inmates that I was present and wandering at irregular times about the prison could act as a restraint on their behaviour. In practice, some such effect probably occurred, but I was around the prison long enough to make it difficult to keep up any consistent practice (even if such were desired).

4. THE STRUCTURE OF THE INTERVIEWS
WITH MEMBERS OF THE SAMPLES

The initial interviews with both staff and inmates followed preconstructed interview guides directed at biographical background information (family and career history), present life situation, and those attitudes and beliefs that I thought to be relevant to the proposed changes. The follow-up interviews in December 1958 were also formally conducted but focused on present situation and

I

attitudes towards the various aspects of the change. Subsequent interviews in March 1959 and February 1960 were conducted on the job, i.e. wherever the officer could be found in the prison with the freedom to discuss the experiment.

One potential difficulty arose concerning interviews of inmates. It seemed very likely that inmates would not tell the truth about matters concerning their own criminality and fairly likely that they would be so biased in their view of the official prison world as to be misleading. Several counter-measures were decided upon and followed in each inmate interview.

(a) The official file on an inmate was not consulted until after the first interview. It was felt that pre-knowledge of the files would tend to be communicated to the inmate in any lengthy interview on the matters proposed. If the inmate sensed this, he would be less likely to believe the stated purpose of the interview and more likely to become defensive about his personal life and beliefs.

(b) The stated purpose of the interview was 'to help us understand the relative value of two ways of running a prison. It was not in any way concerned with helping (or hurting) any particular individual whether inmate or officer'. Simple statement of this purpose was not enough: the inmates acted as if any interview by officialdom or by persons officially introduced into the prison was always concerned with their personal affairs. More detail about the purpose helped, but conviction was only conveyed by other measures.

Connected with this suspicion of the stated purposes was the question invariably asked in the first interviews, 'Why pick me out?' An explanation was given of the sampling procedure and assurances given that neither the governor nor anyone else of the staff had had any say in the choice of inmates.

(c) The most important measure taken in the individual interview to convince the inmate of the purpose was in fact to centre the questions on matters of prison life and organization. Each inmate had had considerable experience of these things – in many cases running back to Approved Schools. The procedure adopted was to go through these experiences in their temporal order again and again, each time focusing on a different aspect and seeking considerable detail.

As expected, the inmates became more forthcoming each time round, consciously dropping 'stories' earlier put forward and going into matters earlier glided over. Personal background hardly touched on in the first outline of their prison experience (e.g. what happened between sentences and what happened to friends and relations while in prison) was voluntarily brought forward later. (The interview records were subsequently checked in detail against files and, in some cases, with persons who knew the inmates' careers. The correlation correspondence was excellent.)

(d) Measures taken in the individual interviews were not expected to be sufficient. For many of the inmates, the purposes of the study were likely to be too abstract to be grasped, and their own defences too strong to enable them to rely on a personal judgement of the honesty of the interviewer. It was necessary to get some sanction from within the inmate population. The procedure adopted was to identify an inmate in the sample who could give sanction, i.e. whose word that it was 'on the level' would carry weight and be communicated to other inmates. The man selected was employed in the main workshop. For the first three days, inmates of no particular standing were selected from this shop. It was assumed that this would enable some story, however confused, to get back to the leading inmate. We were fortunate in that this man had a friend in the sample who was above average intelligence and personally popular. He was interviewed on the fourth day and particular attention was given to explaining the purposes, the sampling, the conditions of confidence, and the intent behind the questions. On the next day the leading inmate was seen. He proved to be interested and cooperative. The subsequent interviews were with two exceptions markedly easier; the inmates were co-operative and failed to ask 'Why me?' The two exceptions were men who were isolates in the prison community.

Appendix III · Reclassification of disciplinary incidents

In the prison records, all reported offences by inmates are classified according to the regulation reputedly broken. This classification was found to be inadequate for the purposes of this study, and all the incidents were reclassified according to a set of categories which I felt to be psychologically more meaningful. The reclassification was first done on the basis of the recorded evidence of both the officer bringing the charge and the offender; and then, wherever there was any possible doubt, the incident was explored further with informants.

The new classification required that the offender or offenders and their immediate purpose in the offending action should be identified.

The primary distinction was drawn between:

A. events arising from an inmate's seeking his own advantage or entertainment in ways seen by the staff as contravening prison rules (i.e. arising from personal forces directed to increasing one's space of free movement).

B. events arising from the inmate's apparent unwillingness to submit to staff orders or from his attack upon staff authority (i.e. personal forces arising in response to an external pressure or challenge).

Two classificatory problems arise at this point. First, acts officially classed as destructive are sometimes directed primarily against authority in the sense of smashing up those things that belong to 'them'. In other cases, such as restyling prison clothes, the intention is conversion of prison property to one's own uses, not destruction. This distinction has been recognized by some officers in making out their reports, putting the former under rule 9 and the latter under rule 19. Others, notably the stricter ones, appear to insist that all destruction is indirectly aimed at their authority (i.e. is a contravention of rule 9). From the evidence given at the governor's hearing, it is usually possible to distinguish these.

The second classificatory problem concerned events in which the prisoner had tried to trick an officer into granting a privilege for which, under the rules, he was not due. These are here judged as going beyond Class A events, in that they imply a willingness to subvert the authority of an officer, and hence are classed as Class B events.

The next stage in the classification was to distinguish between two subclasses of incidents within both A and B:

A. I. events arising from isolated individual actions to gain privileges (e.g. unlawful possessions, smoking),

   II. events arising from joint actions or from attempting to establish relations with other prisoners (e.g. horseplay, shouting out together, bartering, and fighting),

B. III. unwillingness to perform required duties (e.g. self-care, cleaning cell, observing work discipline, work norms, and movement discipline),

   IV. acting so as to challenge or undermine staff authority (e.g. poking fun at, abusing, threatening, or striking officers, spiteful destruction of prison property, tricking an officer into wrong actions, and blatant disobedience of an order given to the inmate personally).

Although my classification differs from that used by the staff in the ways mentioned above, the two are significantly related in making the primary distinction.

Table 1 – Relation between my categories and those used by the staff *

	A I & II	B III & IV	
Rules 6, 8, 11, 12, 16, 18, 19	159	31	190
Rules 1, 2, 3, 4, 9, 10	42	146	188
	201	177	378†

(* For incidents reported in the period fourteen weeks before change and twenty-three after.)

(† 3 cases came under rule 20 'attempts any of these')

$$(\emptyset = 0.66 \ p < .001)$$

The distinction between categories I and II is relevant for administration, in that the latter are more prejudicial to good order but, for the most part, the two kinds of events are classified by the staff under rule 19. The distinction between III and IV is of greater administrative relevance, and some correspondence exists between the way the rules are used and our classification.

Table 2 – Relation between categories
III & IV and rules 1, 4, 9

	Category		
	I & II	III	IV
Rule 1	29	43	10
4	—	10	51
9	10	—	10

This classification also bears some relation to the stringency of punishments allotted. As shown by the following table, the different types of events seem to evoke different punishments.

Table 3 – Relation between my classification and punishments meted out

	Class of events				
Form of punishment	I	II	III	IV	
Loss of remission or referral to V.C.*	7	10	17	24	58
C.C. and No. 1 diet†	1	9	19	16	45
Loss of earnings or assoc.	16	26	18	10	70
	24	45	54	50	173

$$\chi^2 = 24\cdot99 \quad p < \cdot001 \quad C = 0\cdot32$$

* Visiting Committee of Magistrates.
† Solitary confinement on restricted diet.

The severity of punishment in this sample of incidents is significantly related to the order of seriousness theoretically attached to the classification.

Author Index

Subject Index